PATTE

of th

SACRED

English Protestant and Russian Orthodox
Pilgrims of the Nineteenth Century

*To all who have travelled and will travel
to Jerusalem with the spirit and
the soul of a pilgrim*

PATTERNS

of the

SACRED

English Protestant and Russian Orthodox
Pilgrims of the Nineteenth Century

Ruth and Thomas Hummel

Swedish Christian Study Centre, Jerusalem

SCORPION
CAVENDISH

Front Cover: Throngs of pilgrims crowding every nook and cranny of the parvis of the Holy Sepulchre during Easter Week celebrations

© Ruth and Thomas Hummel and
the Swedish Christian Study Centre, Jerusalem, 1995

This publication was made possible through the support and generosity of the Swedish Christian Study Centre, Jerusalem.

First published in 1995 by
Scorpion Cavendish Ltd
31 Museum Street
London WC1A 1LH
England

ISBN 1 900269 08 2

Editor: Leonard Harrow
Design: Knowles Thompson PLC, London WC1
Printed and bound in England by Butler & Tanner Limited, Frome

Acknowledgements

From the beginning of this project we have been blessed with the support, co-operation and goodwill of many people and institutions. The Swedish Christian Study Centre in Jerusalem has generously supported us in a variety of ways from providing a forum for an initial lecture on the subject to financing the writing and publication of this text; to them and to the three directors in Jerusalem with whom we have worked our most heartfelt thanks. We are also indebted to Episcopal High School and Holton-Arms School which provided sabbatical opportunities and the Master and Fellows of Peterhouse College, Cambridge, which provided an institutional home during part of the research and writing of this text. George Hintlian of the Armenian Patriarchate in Jerusalem served as the intellectual mentor to both of us – navigating us through the Christian Holy Land and giving us an appreciation of its wonders. Bishop Theophanus, superior of the Greek Orthodox monastery in Bethlehem, read the text and offered a number of helpful suggestions as did Perry Epes who also did an extensive editorial diagnosis. Henry Chadwick and Derick Hopwood gave of their special expertise on Greek translations and Russian political interests in 19th century Jerusalem respectively. George Hobart and Cheryl Regan of the Library of Congress, Washington, DC, and the Citadel Museum of Jerusalem graciously contributed professional advice and photography. Bill Brown of McLean, Virginia and Bishop Kapekian and Metropolitan Daniel of Jerusalem were tireless contributors of ideas and encouragement.

Ruth and Thomas Hummel

Preface

The idea for this book was born in the Holy Sepulchre on Palm Sunday 1991, as the Greek Orthodox Patriarch made his second perambulation around the Anastasis (Holy Sepulchre). The hostilities of the Gulf War which had ended but a few weeks before greatly diminished the numbers of pilgrims witnessing this re-enactment of Christ's triumphal entry into the Holy City.

So I stood in relative comfort with my back against one of the Crusader columns encircling the edicule, the rectangular structure of marble cocooning the tomb of Christ. I stood there as a participant and an observer thinking of the difference between the staid solemn Palm Sunday processions of my Episcopal Church in America and this joyous sometimes riotous gathering before me of hardy Greek and Cypriot pilgrims. The ranks of local Christians swelled by these pilgrims vied ardently to catch a piece of an olive branch or a sprig of rosemary cast upon the congregation by the procession

My reflections were suddenly interrupted by a Mid-Western American twang asking, 'Do you speak English? Can you tell me what's going on here?' I looked up to see a tall slightly balding middle-aged man. 'Well, what exactly would you like to know?', I responded. 'Well, what are they doing? Why are all these people pushing each other?' He must have sensed my hesitation because a business card was quickly produced which introduced him as a consultant to several Protestant Christian charitable organizations.

'Well, the Greek Orthodox, Armenians, Syrians and Copts are taking turns re-enacting Christ's triumphal entry into Jerusalem. Each process three times around the tomb. Now the Greek patriarch is finishing his second pilgrimage.' I stated this with complete authority since I had been briefed several days before by an Armenian friend on the protocol of the Holy Week services.

'Yeh, I know it's Palm Sunday but what does this carnival have to do with religion?' His question was absolutely sincere. For him this was a 'carnival' of shoving pilgrims and embattled prelates trying to push through the crowd. He had come to the Holy Sepulchre for contemplative Palm Sunday inspiration but had found chaos and cacophony.

I was angry that he was disturbing my Palm Sunday meditations and I was angry that I had no ready three-minute cogent argument to explain the antique beauty, the theological rationale or the spirituality of those Greek and Cypriot pilgrims.

I uttered some generalities about re-enacting Christ's entry but he could read my uneasiness and knew that I did not want to speak with him. Before he left he deposited in my hand a few bits of what seemed to be rock fragments from a plastic bag he pulled from the pocket of his tweed jacket. 'This is special frankincense I bought here. I want you to have a few pieces,' he said quitely. I was touched by his gift but relieved when he drifted to some other corner of the Holy Sepulchre.

As the Armenian patriarch under branches of an olive tree began his progress around the tomb of Christ, I continued to think about the Mid-Westerner's reaction to the procession of sumptuous robes, banners and enthused Christians brushing pass me and I thought about what I was witnessing and my own reactions.

Adjacent to the courtyard of the Church of the Holy Sepulchre is the market of Aftimos, a place of cafes, souvenir and leather shops. Here in a cafe I sat and watched the pious solemn Protestants coming from the Easter services of the Lutheran Church of the Redeemer (Orthodox Palm Sunday was Western Easter this year) mixing with the steady stream of black-clad Orthodox pilgrims coming from the Holy Sepulchre. Two different worlds were brushing against one another – two Christian traditions sharing the same space but not communicating. It was then that I decided to investigate how the West and the East interpreted the celebration of Easter in the Holy Land. Being an historian I sought answers in the past.

The opportunity to explore this issue in depth came when my husband, an ecclesiastical historian and Anglican priest, took an interest in the subject just as he acquired the time (a sabbatical), the resources (a fellowship in Cambridge) and the incentive (a lecture invitation in Jerusalem). The researching and writing took place primarily during that time. The finished project merges his interests in the theological theme of the sacramentality of pilgrimage with my interests in the more sociological and personal devotional aspects. We were also able to draw upon my work on early photography in Palestine to illustrate this book with appropriate photographs from the period. This is truly a joint effort which drew upon the many years we have both spent in the Holy Land watching it struggle with contemporary problems while studying its turbulent history. It is also our attempt to help assist the different Christian pilgrims who visit the Holy Land to come to better understand not only the origins of their faith but their fellow Christians as well.

Ruth Victor Hummel
Feast of the Assumption
Jerusalem, 1995

Contents

List of Plates

8   Russian pilgrims bathe with their white shrouds in the holy waters of the Jordan River. It was considered a great honour to be buried with shrouds sanctified in the river where Christ himself was baptized

9   Bethlehem residents in their traditional costumes intermingled with pilgrims awaiting the arrival of the Christmas procession in Manger Square

10   In 1894 clergyman, Bishop Vincent, usually a critic of Orthodox piety, annotated the above photo, ' . . . Before us [is] a recess where fifteen lamps are suspended, six belonging to the Greeks, five to the Armenians and four to the Latins. And in the floor of a recess a silver star is placed in the pavement of which are these words: *Hic de Virginie Maria Jesus Christus Natus est.* Here let all prejudices for the moment vanish, and let us observe the reverent manner of the worshippers. Whatever else they believe in they believe in Christ, the Babe, the Man, the Deity incarnate.'

11   Pilgrim Greek clergy holding crosses in front of the Holy Sepulchre

12   Protestant American pilgrims on the outskirts of Jerusalem, leaving for an excursion accompanied by local escorts

13   In 1894 the author of *Earthly Footsteps of the Man of Galilee* wrote about his photo, 'Travellers now ride on English saddles and on excellent horses, sleeping at night in carpeted tents most comfortably furnished.'

14   'Inside the Garden of Gethsemane the Eastern churches have placed . . . the "stations" representing the various incidents of the crucifixion. We [Protestant pilgrims] were here during the Greek Easter week, and many pilgrims were making the rounds of the "stations" in the garden.' Note the city walls and the Golden Gate in the background

15　　　Special pilgrim boats sailing out to pick up pilgrims from the ships anchored beyond the forbidding rocks of Jaffa harbour. Note the name *Rolla Floyd* on the bow. Floyd was one of the most popular dragomen for English and American pilgrims and tourists

16　　　Russian pilgrims resting on the way to the Jordan River

17　　　Protestant pilgrims on the banks of the Jordan River

18　　　Encampment of Protestant pilgrims

19　　　This photo entitled, 'The Lord is my Shepherd', from the Twenty Third Psalm series of the American Colony studio in Jerusalem beautifully depicts how the Protestant pilgrim wanted to experience the Holy Land – a Palestine untouched by the passage of almost two millennia

20　　　The oak at Mamre was a favourite site for the Russian pilgrim who knew the story of Abraham and his three holy guests from some of the most well-loved Orthodox icons

21　　　A bit of the Holy Fire safely housed in a lantern for its journey to Mother Russia

22　　　Russian pilgrims with their banners on their way to the Jordan River

23　　　A Russian pilgrim triumphantly dries his shroud on a cane cut from a bush along the bank of the Jordan River

24　　　Local inhabitants pose outside of the site tradition sanctions as the tomb of Lazarus. Although they remarked that this site was 'but a tradition', Protestant pilgrims believed 'the strong possibility . . . that the tomb is not very far away.'

25   The entrance into the Life-Giving Tomb within the Church of the Resurrection (Holy Sepulchre). This is the enhanced glorified tomb so familiar to Russian Pilgrims from their icons

26   'The tomb of our Lord, "The New Calvary", outside of Jerusalem.' This is Gordon's tomb outside of Damascus gate accepted by some Protestants as the more probable site of Christ's entombment in accord with their desire to discover the authentic unembellished Redeemer. (Note the photographer's addition of the two women to intensify the identification with the gospel account.)

Photographic Credits

Numbers refer to those assigned to each photograph. Page numbers refer to quotes used in a caption.

Prints and Photographs Division, Library of Congress: Cover, 6, 8, 9, 11

Matson Collection, Prints and Photographs Division, Library of Congress: 7, 16, 19, 20, 25

Stephen Graham, *With the Russian Pilgrims to Jerusalem*, Macmillan, London, 1913: 21, 22, 23

Collections of the Archives for Historical Documentation, Brighton, Massachusetts: 12

John Barnier Collection at the Archives for Historical Documentation, Brighton, Massachusetts: 17,18

John H Vincent, *Earthly Footsteps of the Man of Galilee,* N D Thompson, New York, 1894, p. 31 (10), p. 137 (13), p. 246 (14), p. 264 (15), p. 229 (24)

Tower of David/Museum of the History of Jerusalem: 1, 2, 3, 4, 5

Hummel Photographic Collection, stereoscope from Underwood & Underwood: 26

The Bible Lands

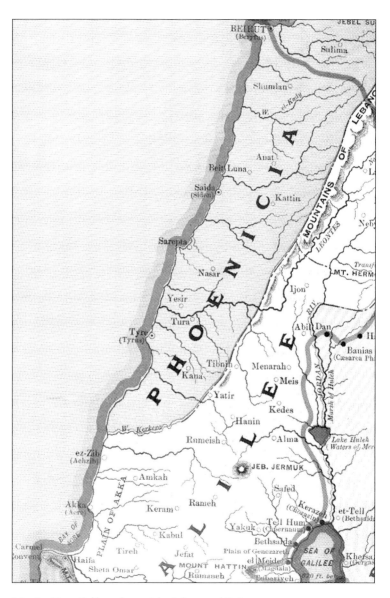

Map I   *Upper Galilee and present day Lebanon and Syria*

Tracing the pilgrimage route of the authors and photographer of *Earthly Footsteps of the Man of Galilee*

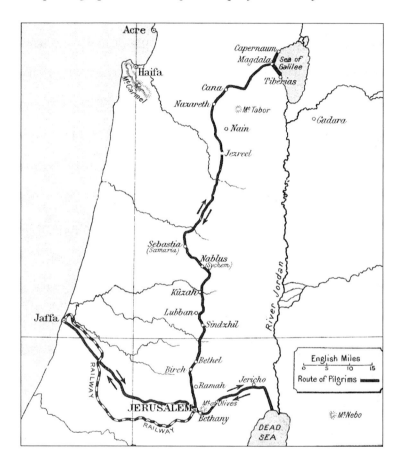

Map II   *Biblical lands of Samaria, Judea, Moab and Peraea*

Introduction

For almost two millennia Christians have travelled to Jerusalem and the Holy Land in search of the roots of their faith. They have also expected it to affirm their community's doctrinal beliefs and liturgical practices while re-enforcing its claim to represent the truly apostolic Church. Yet frequently their spiritual patrimony, the land of Jesus, would appear to them disturbingly unfamiliar. It would then be a quest for these Christians and their churches to try and make Jerusalem and the Holy Sites speak in the language of their tradition. Primarily through pilgrimage and diplomacy, but occasionally through conquest, they sought to stamp their vision on the city where Jesus died and was resurrected and the land where he was born and preached. The land, however, belonged to a people whose culture was not Christian but whose reverence for the place was equally rooted in sacred memory and as such resisted transformation into the image of the pilgrims. Even the exclusively Christian sites spoke in the ambiguous voice of contending traditions. This is the story of two Christian communities, the English Protestants and the Russian Orthodox, who in the nineteenth century sought the faith-bolstering experience of visiting the Holy Land, and of what they expected and what they encountered and (in the case of the Protestants) what effect the presence of the Orthodox had on them.

With the increase in Western interest and presence in nineteenth century Palestine, two groups stand out – the English Protestants and the Russian Orthodox pilgrims – because of their numbers or influence, the religious focus of their aims, and the implicit or explicit imperialism of their ventures. Many other groups, sects and individuals came during this time, of course, and some have left lasting monuments in stone or memory, but these two provide an interesting contrast on both the political and theological level. It will be our contention that these two communities clash with each other because of their differing visions of Jerusalem and their respective ideas of sacramentality. This is therefore a fascinating conflict of Eastern and Western Christianity in the context of the larger cultural clash of the Orient with the Occident.

For both the English Protestants and the Russian Orthodox, two factors combined to bring forth pilgrims in unprecedented numbers. The first factor was political and the second technological. For the English the political factor was manifested in the increased interest in Egypt and Palestine as part of a growing commercial and political empire connecting Britain to India. With Napoleon's expedition to the Near East in 1798 and then the completion of the Suez Canal in 1869, the British became aware of the need to stake a claim to the land through which their lifeline to India now flowed. The growing weakness of the Ottoman empire also meant that this area was increasingly viewed as becoming available to Western colonization and the British empire did not want other powers, notably France or Russia, to challenge their hegemony. This increased British presence in the Near East, especially Egypt, meant that it was now easier to visit the Holy Land for religious purposes from a secure British base. This was especially true after the Egyptian Muhammad Ali's conquest of Palestine in 1831 provided greater access to the Holy Sites. Though in 1840 the area reverted to the Ottomans, with Western help, this opening up of Jerusalem to the West continued. It coincided with the second, technological factor of an improved transportation network. Railroads and steamships made travel to foreign lands much more accessible. Although the conditions of travel within Palestine did not improve markedly until late in the century, with the Jaffa to Jerusalem railroad in 1892, the means to travel there in relative comfort and at reasonable cost, and the development of travel organizations like Thomas Cook's tour made visiting a realistic option for those who had the leisure, interest and resources – in fact a rather large number.

By 1882 Cook's Tours alone had facilitated over 5,000 visitors, mostly British, to come to the Holy Land [*Thomas Cook*, Brendon, p. 139]. The Cook organization catered to middle-class clients who wanted their exotica to be packaged and for whom a certain degree of comfort was requisite. The travellers' comfort may have been relative, but it was a huge improvement over earlier times. The food especially was imported to give a taste of home, and on at least one trip bottled beer was insisted upon, although it burst in the heat. Cook's also successfully segregated their clients from the natives and the Russian peasants. While in Palestine they camped in tents, thereby avoiding hotels and hostels and enabling them to stay with their own kind. Similarly Cook's provided men's and women's bathing tents at the Jordan; as a result "English travellers no longer had to plunge into the Jordan with half naked Russian peasants" [Shepherd, p. 177].

The Russians also had a long history of interest in the Holy Land. As early as 1689 Patriarch Dositheos of Jerusalem tried to win the support of Russia in his fight against the sultan's 'betrayal' of the Holy Places into Latin hands. As a result the Russians realized how their political ambitions could be furthered by their role as defender of Orthodox interests. Consequently the relationship between the Russian Church and the rest of Eastern Orthodoxy increasingly became lodged in the foreign ministry [Stavrou p. 16-17]. In the early nineteenth century the Treaty of Adrianople, ending the Russo-Turkish War of 1828-29, recognized Russia as the guardian of the Orthodox population in the Ottoman empire. This diplomatic opening was used to expand Russia's presence in Palestine with a consulate established in Jaffa, some pilgrimage facilities organized in Jerusalem, and a school for Arab children. The Crimean War (1853-56) led to a temporary slackening of efforts, but the creation of the Palestine Committee under Grand Duke Konstatin Nikolaevich, with foreign ministry support, meant a renewed effort. In the years 1858-1864 the committee had created a pilgrim's hostel in Jerusalem, built its cathedral outside the city walls, established an ecclesiastical mission with a permanent staff, and founded a hospital. This committee was replaced in 1882 by the Russian Orthodox Palestine Society. Its mission was to encourage pilgrims, provide guides and guidebooks for the Russians in their own language, and develop Russian language services at the holy sites, as well as organize transportation to and within the Holy Land. The society was especially successful in the latter task. Special pilgrimage rates were secured from railroads and steamship lines, reducing the cost of the journey by half and thereby increasing the number of pilgrims dramatically. While in 1877 only 35 Russians made the pilgrimage, by 1884 they had increased to over 2,000 and by 1900 there were more than 7,000 Russian pilgrims [Stavrou p. 150,183]. As in the case of the British, the political agenda was reinforced by the religious desire for pilgrimage and aided by the technological development of railroads, steamships and infrastructure. The Russians came on a massive scale, and most writers of the period vividly remember the large groups of black-clad Russian peasants streaming through the streets of Jerusalem at Easter. What each of these Protestants and Russians thought of the Holy Land and of each other is the essence of this story.

We want to look at each of these two groups in turn and ask a number of questions: Who were they? Why did they go to the Holy Land? What did they do when they got there? What were their expectations and how were these realized or disappointed? What significance did the Holy Land have for their religious life? and What were their political agendas?

English Protestants

Who were they?

Based upon a survey of those who wrote about their visit to the Holy Land, the most common type of English visitor who came for predominantly religious purposes was a clergyman, usually of the broad church or evangelical wing of the Church of England or a member of one of the dissenting Protestant Churches. These were often accompanied by family and friends who presumably held similar views and prejudices. There were also a large number of educated and pious laypeople who came for a mixture of religion and romance, a taste of the biblically familiar and the exotic East.

A cross section of the sources used in this book exemplifies the variety of circumstances which led to the trip. The Revd Joseph Thomas from Oxford, author of *Oxford to Palestine*, had already written one successful travel book and made another volume out of letters which he sent back to the *Oxford Times*, possibly subsidizing his journey. Reginald Hertslet was a foreign office official who travelled for reasons of health, hoping to recover from a serious illness. His trip he found both spiritually and physically rehabilitating. The Revd William Jowett went out to the Holy Land as a representative of the Church Missionary Society to investigate the prospects and to design an infiltration strategy. One of the more interesting characters was the Revd James Cuthbertson, a Wesleyan minister who in his introduction explains how he got the opportunity to make his pilgrimage. As a young man he worked for the estate manager of the Marchioness of Londonderry, George Elliot, who summoned the young man and offered him a better position. Cuthbertson refused, saying he was going to study to be a minister. Twenty years later Sir George Elliot, now knighted and an MP, heard Cuthbertson preach at his church in Whitby and offered him the trip as a gift. William Leighton, who took a Cook's Tour, was an accountant who wanted to escape business concerns and whose childhood involvement in the Sandemanian sect had left him with a love of scripture. Charles Warner tells of the shoemaker from the south of England whose lifetime savings bought him a tour ticket. Such working-class presence was rare, as the comment which it elicits makes clear.

Early in the century these pilgrims tended to be people on their way to other destinations or on expeditions to improve their health. As the ease of travel increased and rise of the travel industry began to be felt, more and more travellers were interest groups such as the Sunday School Teachers tour or one of Mr Thomas Cook's tours. According to the letters of William Leighton describing a Cook's Tour of 1874, the clientele divided evenly between British and American, clergy and laity. The clergy were Methodists and Baptists as well as Anglicans, while the laity were a young dissenting couple, two 'spinster sisters', and a number of men of varying piety. All, however, were avidly Protestant in their rejection of Catholic and Greek 'superstition', and Western in their critical and sceptical view of the Holy Place [*A Cook's Tour To The Holy Land*]. Naomi Shepherd describes the nature of these Cook Tours as combining "visits to the Holy Places, the missions and their schools, and biblical excavations; the parties carried not only maps and guide books but bibles and hymn books and sang as they went" [*Zealous Intruders*, p. 181].

The literary, academic, and political luminaries were also frequent visitors and even more frequent commentators on the experience. It was often their observations which most shaped the attitudes of British readers and subsequent pilgrims. Kinglake's *Eothen*, Curzon's *Visits to Monasteries in the Levant*, Bartlett's *Walks About the City and Environs of Jerusalem*, and Dean Stanley's *Sinai and*

Palestine are notable examples. The conclusion seems to be that these English Protestant pilgrims were predominantly of the educated upper and middle classes and that they shared a strong background in the Bible-centred religious upbringing of the Protestant section of the Church of England or another Protestant church as well as Victorian moral and political values. The high church or Anglo-Catholic wing of Anglicanism was not well represented on these pilgrimages. When the Catholic Anglicans did go, their attitude was much more sympathetic to the Roman and Greek Churches so the expression 'Protestant' to describe the other pilgrims is appropriate. The High Church Anglicans did, however, share the political, social and economic views of their Protestant compatriots.

Why do they visit the Holy Land?

For the English pilgrims who made the trip during the nineteenth century there was usually the allure of the exotic adventure in the excursion. It had long been a part of the 'education' of the upper-classes to have a Grand Tour to the cultural sites of Europe, and the Romantic Movement with its invocation of ancient glories and appreciation of picturesque ruins gave an added impetus to the journey. With greater accessibility in terms of comfort and cost, the less nobly endowed could partake in the experience as well. And if communion with the ruins of Greece and Rome could bestow such wondrous blessings as those described by Byron, how much more ennobling to the soul would be the view of the very land where God had enacted His sacred history. The Revd Cuthbertson expressed this sentiment when he wrote how the classical sights are wonderful and instructive and celebrated by great works of literature, but 'the imperishable interest attaching to Palestine does not rest upon such a foundation as these. It is the land chosen by God as a sanctuary' [Cuthbertson, p. 42]. So the pilgrims set off to see the sites where the Bible took place with the expectation that the experience would both expand their understanding of scripture and deepen their faith. The accessibility of the Holy Land did create some problems because, as we have seen, it was occasionally possible for a member of the labouring class to join a Cook's Tour. Such a situation meant an uncomfortableness about how to relate to a person as both a fellow traveller and social inferior. As the journeys progressed, however, the enthusiasm and biblical knowledge of these working-class lay preachers usually overcame the class distinctions.

There were, of course, the mere adventurers looking for exotic people, places, and events to add to their after dinner speeches, and the imperialistic and individualistic exploiters for political or commercial profit, but these we will avoid as falling outside the category of pilgrims. If the mere adventurers represent one extreme, the 'scientific' and professional cleric represents the other. Some of these went to the Holy Land in order to complete their education. Philip Schaff of the Union Theological Seminary in New York suggested that every student who could secure the funds should travel to the Bible lands to complement his academic training. 'It will be of more practical use to him in his pulpit labours than the lectures of the professors in Oxford or Cambridge, in Berlin or Leipzig . . . ' (Notably, his own city of New York is not mentioned.) A minister who has experienced the Holy Land will fill 'his memory with a gallery of photographic pictures more valuable than a number of books.' From then on the mere mention of Jerusalem, Nazareth, Bethlehem, Gethsemane and these places will 'rise up before his mental eyes with a vividness which they never had before' [Schaff, p. 14-15]. Another type of 'scientific' approach is represented by the American Revd Henry Osborn, who decided to do a detailed analysis of the soil of the Holy Land to demonstrate that it is fertile and could support the luxurious crops described in the Bible. He identifies fifteen components in the holy soil [Osborn, p. 276].

This study will focus on the first type of expert, those who sought exegetical tools but avoided the large number of biblical scientists and archaeologists who were intent upon proving the Bible to be true through the auspices of the very scientific techniques which were undermining its authority in the West. The Palestine Exploration Fund and its work seems to stand between these two types or to have its foot in both camps.

There was one group, however, whose journeys were an inseparable combination of pilgrimage and imperialism, and those were the church officials and missionaries. Their brief was not only to visit the Holy Land but to transform it – to convert its populace to Protestant Christianity by building Protestant churches, to introduce Western ideas of hygiene by establishing hospitals, and to inculcate English political, social, moral and economic values by erecting schools.

These Protestant pilgrims were, therefore, mostly drawn to see the land of the Bible for the inspiration and edification it could bring. But they were also members of a society with great confidence in the superiority of its physical as well as spiritual culture, and these attitudes exhibited themselves strongly in their accounts. They mostly travelled as pilgrims, but they were not blind to the social, economic, political as well as religious factors present in Palestine and to the state of the indigenous population. When they came as missionaries they worked to change these conditions, and when they were mere pilgrims they supported the missionaries' work. In their writings they offer acute observations of the cultural as well as physical landscape, although always filtered through the lens of their own culture and religion.

What did the Protestants do when they came to the Holy Land?

The itinerary of the English Protestant pilgrims was much more varied at the beginning of the century than at the end, primarily because of the development of the proto-package tour. The earlier and more adventurous visitors frequently came overland from Egypt, visiting Sinai and other biblical sites on the way to Jerusalem. This was more time consuming, physically taxing, and expensive and was, therefore, an infrequent and more exotic route. The normal journey involved a sea voyage to the 'port' of Jaffa where, because there was no real harbour, the passengers were loaded onto small rowboats and brought ashore. This was one of the most dangerous aspects of the trip, and there are frequent accounts of people drowned as this transfer of human cargo was attempted in rough seas. The advice of Mrs. King, the sister of Dr Liddon, was to pretend to be a sack of potatoes and go limp and let the sailors toss one about. The elderly Dr Liddon found such passivity difficult, and as a result of his thrashing about, almost ended up a victim [Mrs King, *Dr Liddon's Tour*]. The Revd Thomas in his book tells about the Arab boatmen fighting over customers, each trying to pull the passenger into his rowboat. So even if the sea were calm, as it was for him, the trip to Jaffa could be dangerous.

This introduction to the Holy Land seemed *apropos* to a number of authors who saw this chaotic disembarkation as a severing of one's last links to the West and its comforts. The act of being tossed into small boats commanded by strangely dressed Arabs became a real rite of passage into the exotic world of the East. Once on shore the onslaught of sellers, beggars, and agents for various services, from hotels to hire camels, seems to have combined with the heat, smells, and dust to induce a cultural vertigo. The advice was to locate immediately a trustworthy dragoman – either one provided by the tour organizer or one recommended by previous visitors. Once a dragoman was obtained, it would then be his job to do all the negotiations necessary to find lodgings and hire the horses and supplies for the trek up to Jerusalem. It was a frequent complaint from travellers that dragomen would agree on a price and then, once the journey began, demand more to go on, leaving the client in an impossible situation. This reputed unreliability provided Thomas Cook with one of his most valuable selling points. His tours were pre-paid, with meals, lodgings, and guides all included, and attracted all sorts and conditions from the humble shoemaker to Mark Twain and the Emperor of Germany.[*Thomas Cook: 150 Years of Popular Tourism*]

As the century progressed the journey from Jaffa to Jerusalem became easier and more comfortable. Initially it would take two to three days, with overnight stays in one of the convents along the way – in Ramleh for example. Before the bandit clan of Abu Gosh was suppressed by the Turks around 1846, this trip usually included an unscheduled stop in the village's territory, during which a tariff was collected by the villagers. This involuntary baksheesh greatly resembled highway robbery and could be avoided by having Turkish soldiers as escorts. The colourful outfits of the dragomen along with the antics of the soldiers escorting the groups made for a rather fair-like atmosphere. The Cook's Tour people would all be recognized as they sauntered along at a measured pace, with pack animals carrying kitchens clattering behind the column.

> The road is thronged with pilgrims to Jerusalem . . . All the transport of freight as well as passengers is by the backs of beasts of burden. There are long files of horses and mules staggering under enormous loads of trunks, tents and bags. Dragomans, some of them got up in fierce style, with baggy trousers, yellow kuffias bound about the head with a twisted fillet, armed with long Damascus swords, their belts stuck full of pistols, and a rifle slung on the back, gallop furiously along the line, the signs of danger but the assurance of protection. Camp boys and waiters dash along also, on the pack-horses, with a great clatter of kitchen furniture, even a scullion has an air of adventure as he pounds his rack-a-bone steed into a vigorous gallop. And there are the Cook's tourists, called by everybody "cookies", men and women struggling on according to the pace of their horses, conspicuous in hats with white muslin drapery hanging over the neck [Werner, *In the Levant,* p. 19].

Many travellers looked down upon these 'Cookies' who were thought to wallow in unmitigated luxury. But as William Leighton complained:

> The sleeping tents are circular: the two married couples have a tent each, the two Miss Ledgers have one, and the rest of us are stowed 3 in a tent. Each tent contains three iron bedsteads with not very comfortable beds, with a table with tin jug and wash basins. These with portmanteaus fill the tent, and there are two difficulties: first where to put your clothes, secondly where to find

them in the morning. There is not room to wash so we
don't attempt it [Leighton, p. 52].

In fact one of his party washed so infrequently that he was
known as the odoriferous Gale. They ate in a large saloon tent of
about 25ft by 15ft which was supplied by a kitchen in a tent of
almost equal size. The food was imported with the tour and
consisted of tea and coffee, potted salmon, bacon and Yorkshire
ham, and lots of fruit. That was breakfast. Lunch and dinner were
much the same. But the luxuriousness was only relative to what
others endured; on the trip chronicled by William Leighton,
everyone was seriously ill at some stage with fever, and one man, the
infamous Gale, died [Leighton, p. 52].

In the 1880s the journey from Jaffa to Jerusalem could be
accomplished by carriage in 9 hours, as it was by the Revd Thomas
[Thomas, p. 68]. By the 1890s this same journey along the Plain of
Sharon and up the hills to Jerusalem was completed in a few hours
by rail. Those who travelled both ways lamented the ease of the rail
journey; it was a spiritual loss, they felt, not to view Jerusalem first,
and then finally attain the city only after an arduous series of hills
and valleys. There was theological symbolism in the trip because
after a long ascent, the view of the city of God in the distance gave
hope and comfort in the hard journey remaining, just as the
heavenly Jerusalem comforts those who have the vision of faith for
the journey of life. This connection of the pilgrim's journey of faith
had, of course, a deep resonance among the English who, would be
familiar with Bunyan's *Pilgrim's Progress*.

The first glimpses of the object of this trip struck these English
pilgrims in various ways. Some were overcome with the sight of the
walled city with domes glowing – here, they said, is the true earthly
symbol of the kingdom of God. Others mocked the romantics who
broke out into pious exclamations or maudlin tears and saw only a
rather bedraggled small town whose power is not displayed to the
eyes but hidden away, only to be unlocked by those who approach it
with the eyes of faith [Tweedie, p. 10]. The majority had the
ambiguous reaction of seeing the city shimmering in the sun and
being moved but wary of falling into an idolatrous attitude and

mistaking the symbol for what it symbolizes. Especially those who had been prepared for what awaited them inside the walls were hesitant to prostrate their hearts to the town. The tension between the heavenly Jerusalem and the earthly one, which made an important theological point, was also reflected in the tension between the Jerusalem of the Romantic imagination and the reality of a small, rather economically deprived town in the hinterland of the Turkish empire.

Once inside the city those who were initially enamoured of the symbol quickly became aware of the mundane reality. Early in the century the lodgings would have been almost exclusively in the Latin, Greek, or Armenian convents. The Armenian convent was universally viewed as the most clean, modern, and therefore civilized of the lot. By late in the century hotels, hostels, and other facilities became available, giving a wider range of accommodations, although until quite late the 'Cookies' continued to live in tents outside the walls, trusting no native accommodations.

In Jerusalem the English pilgrims were, of course, interested in the whole panoply of sacred sites. The Holy Sepulchre was primary, but the Temple Mount and Dome of the Rock (once they were open to non-Muslims), the Garden of Gethsemane, Mount of Olives, Church of the Ascension, the house of the Last Supper, and the Tomb of the Virgin were all *de rigueur*. The Protestants travelled the Via Dolorosa but did not have the same programmed stations of the cross as the Roman Catholics. For the English Protestants the sites that moved them most were the landscape sites – the Mount of Olives and the Garden of Gethsemane – while they were more distrustful and their reactions more ambiguous towards the traditional Holy Places. Although many English visitors made an effort to be in Jerusalem for Easter, it was not seen as a major bonus, and for some the large numbers of other pilgrims, especially the ubiquitous Russians, made trips at other times of the year preferable.

Once they had successfully 'done' Jerusalem, these peripatetic pilgrims would begin a trip to the major gospel sites, travelling to Bethlehem, Hebron, the Dead Sea (also a natural wonder), Jericho, the Jordan River, Tiberias (to the Lake of Galilee), Nazareth, and Mt Tabor. Other places of historical interest, such as the desert monastery of Mar Saba, the Samaritan community, or Crusader ruins, might also be added in for variety. At each of these sites there were favourite locations which seemed to capture the Protestant imagination and other places which left them unmoved.

Bethlehem was an ambiguous site. Many found the Grotto of the Nativity a likely location for the manger and the grotto itself iconographically acceptable. Others dismissed it as a fraud, finding inspiration in the nearby 'authentic' grotto of St Jerome, whose presence gave sanctity to the complex. The other sites, like the Milk Grotto, were rejected out of hand as tourist traps. The Shepherd's Field in the outskirts of the town, although lacking any definitive proof for its appellation, did give the Protestant imagination a vision of the landscape of the events surrounding the nativity and was, therefore, suitably appreciated. Bethlehem was also known for the beauty of its women, which almost every traveller (usually male) commented upon. The Christian Bethlehemites probably looked the most familiar of the Eastern women in dress, manners and physical appearance (because of some Crusader blood), and in this case familiarity equalled beauty. The same attitude can be seen reflected in English reactions to the sites. Those which were most familiar, and kept their biblical flavour, were the ones which captured the imagination.

In Hebron was the Cave of Machpelah, the burial place of Abraham and Sarah, Isaac and Rebecca, Jacob and Leah, but what these Protestants most commented upon was the hostility and surliness of its Muslim inhabitants. If Christian Bethlehem was familiar and friendly, Islamic Hebron was foreign and sinister. Yet the Oak of Mamre outside of town again marked a dubious but evocative landscape open to imaginative reconstruction.

The Dead Sea may have been a biblical site, but its inclusion on the Protestant itinerary seems to have been more a result of its strange location and properties. It was almost a requirement to test its buoyancy and healing powers as well to comment on the lack of marine life and its location as the lowest spot on earth. Not one Protestant that we read drew the contrast between the fresh water of the Jordan (baptism) with the sterile, salty water of the Dead Sea (death and judgement) which figures among the Russians.

The Jordan River did, of course, elicit from the Protestants thoughts about baptism, but mostly they bathed in its waters to wash off the salt of the Dead Sea or to find relief from the desert heat. Only rarely was their bathing part of a ceremony of re-baptism, although Baptists were an exception. But even 'Cookies' were provided with bottles in order to capture some of the water to take back for family christenings. And there were readings of appropriate texts from the Bible at the site. In fact, this was a major feature of the Protestant pilgrimages. At each of the sites where something biblical had taken place or where the site was mentioned in the Bible, that text would be read along with suitable prayers and hymns. Often, if there was an ordained clergyman on the tour, he would be asked to give a brief, or sometimes not so brief, address on the importance of the events which had taken place at the spot. If there were several clergy in attendance, they tended to take turns.

At Jericho the pilgrims would read the Joshua story of the conquest of the city and listen to a commentary about the land and its being a gift to Israel. They probably also heard of how that gift had been lost through failure to recognize God's Messiah. Here the biblical history and a theological commentary upon that history joined with a contemporary judgement about the condemned status of the land. This emphasis upon the Old Testament as well as the New Testament sites and texts was mostly a Protestant phenomenon. The Russian pilgrims, as we shall see, were attracted to Old Testament sites such as Abraham's Oak at Mamre, but only when it was a part of their iconographic tradition and symbolized a Christian event or doctrine. The Protestants' acquaintance with the Bible as a whole, and especially with its history and geography, meant they had a special interest in and affinity for those Old Testament sites where acts of God in history had taken place. In fact, this stopping off at both New and Old Testament historical and geographical sites and reading from the Bible was one of the earliest forms of Holy Land pilgrimage practised by Origen and Egeria.

The Sea of Galilee was one of the Protestants' favourite spots, not only because it was here that the teaching and preaching of Christ mostly took place, but also because the sites were the landscapes themselves and not buried inside churches and encumbered with encrusted icons and flickering, oily smelling lamps. The seashore where Jesus broke bread and ate fish with the disciples, the lake where Jesus escaped from the crowds and calmed the waves, the hillside of the beatitudes – all these were there in seemingly undiluted form. There Jesus could almost be seen to inhabit the place. Once the ruins of Capernaum were discovered, that also was a place beloved because it was not monumentalized and the site remained 'pure'. The ruins were seen as especially *apropos* because the city was cursed, and to have been destroyed was a sign of God's judgement. As Jesus said: 'And you Capernaum, will you be lifted up to the skies? No, you will go down to the depths. If the miracles that were performed in you had been performed in Sodom, it would have remained to this day. But I tell you that it will be more bearable for Sodom on the day of judgment than for you' [Matthew 11: 23-24].

Equally the lack of a fishing industry (most travellers comment on there being only one or two boats on the whole lake) was a sign of the fall of this place from grace. It was here that seeds of God's Word had been sown, but hard hearts and closed minds failed to recognize it and the seeds bore no fruit. So the landscape was seen as mirroring that failure as well as witnessing to Jesus' life.

The same could not, of course, be said of Nazareth. Along with Bethlehem, this was one of the centres of Christianity in Palestine. Again the manners and dress of the people made them familiar and friendly although the women were not considered as beautiful as those of Bethlehem. What attracted attention, however, were the schools and hospitals which the various Christian communities were building in competition with one other. The Protestants especially were active in this way, and so many pilgrims saw in Nazareth a prelude to the transformation of the whole region into a modern society if only the missionaries' work could continue unabated. The traditional sites in the city – the place of the Annunciation, Mary and Joseph's house, etc. – were mostly rejected as apocryphal and often mocked by the Protestants. But they were enthralled by the Virgin's Fountain because here at the town's well was obviously the place where Mary would have come to draw water and would have most likely brought the baby Jesus, just as the Nazareth's mothers still brought their children. Here, they felt, was an indubitable place where the early life of Jesus was manifested and where the present residents provided an almost theatrical presentation of a beloved scene from the sacred story.

On the outskirts of Nazareth there was an overlook which gave a prospect of the whole of the Galilee. Many of the Protestants imagined that these were the views that kindled in the young Jesus a love for the beauties of the natural world which he would later use to such effect in his preaching. It was a spot where physical beauty and spiritual beauty seemed to intersect:

> I could not help thinking of more sacred eyes which had looked upon these sights and ranged these landscapes; such memories had a subduing effect on me [Cuthbertson, p. 113].

Cuthbertson also visited nearby Cana and commented on the low alcohol content of the local wine, which accounted, he said, for why one never saw anyone drunk in Palestine. Here a Methodist found a way to combine the use of wine in the Bible with the pro-temperance views of his own denomination [Cuthbertson, p. 120].

Within sight of Nazareth was Mt Tabor, which some traditions identified with the Mount of Transfiguration, but many Protestants felt more convinced by the case for Mt Hermon further north. For those with a more extensive program, Caesarea Philippi (Banyas), Mt Hermon, and Damascus were all part of the tour. This allowed the inclusion of a major Pauline site which might be supplemented later by visits to Corinth, Ephesus, etc., on the voyage home. The itinerary of the Cook's Tours tended to be a bit more extensive, including sites in Lebanon on the way to and from Damascus. Also Cook's Tour usually included a trip to the antiquities of Egypt as well. Those whose tour ended with the Galilee would either return to Jerusalem or continue on to Beirut to begin their trip home.

The English Protestant pilgrims, in addition to visiting these Holy Sites, were also interested in placing what they saw around them into their own historical, social, and political as well as religious paradigms. Therefore, they frequently travelled to indigenous villages and talked with those people whose language skills and inclination made them available for interrogation. Often the people they saw and the places they went were determined by where English schools were located, which meant a rather skewed sampling of opinion.

What were their expectations of the Holy Land and how were these realized or disappointed?

When the English Protestants set out on their journeys to the Holy Land, most of them were ambivalent about what they were going to experience. On the one hand, for many this was a trip of a lifetime taking them to a faraway and exotic place. But it was even more a voyage through time, back to the biblical period where they would be able to see the scenes from the Bible, so much a part of their mental baggage, re-vivified in a new and, they hoped, transforming way. On the other hand, as Protestants they were wary of any suggestion that there was virtue or grace inherent in the place itself. It was not the land that was holy, but the holy thoughts and experiences which it could elicit if approached in the appropriate way. And the appropriate way included eliminating any superstitious or idolatrous ideas that treading on the hallowed soil of Palestine sanctified the pilgrim. That sounded dangerously like the indulgence system – in this case, grace bought from God not with donations but with a costly trip [see *Pilgrimage Yesterday and Today*, J G Davies, chapter 2, for a wonderful explication of this matter]. It was also felt that the magnitude of God's presence was not greater in the Holy Land than anywhere else; after all, God resided in the hearts and souls of believers, not in things – neither bread and wine nor rocks and soil. So the Protestant pilgrim strongly rejected any concept of Catholic sacramentality. Most came already warned that they would discover great superstition, idolatry, and fraud perpetrated by dissolute monks who desecrated the Holy Sites with their fanciful rituals. Therefore, it was with an expectation of the illumination of biblical truth, interspersed with the false idols of human error, that these pilgrims confronted the reality of Jerusalem and the surrounding countryside.

It is not surprising that these expectations, reinforced by the theological assumptions of their Bible centred, sacramentally suspicious Protestantism, should be largely realized by their exposure to the Holy Land itself. Most people see and interpret reality based upon their presuppositions, and the English Protestant pilgrims were no exception. For these voyagers from a distant land, most of the traditional Holy Sites were a great disappointment because they found that the 'language' of piety permeating these places – that is, the iconography, the rituals, the pious customs – was foreign. This feeling of being an alien in the home of the Christian gospel was very disconcerting because it called into question the universality, adequacy, and legitimacy of their own view of the Christian religion. If this strange manifestation of seeming mumbo-jumbo was really Christian, then their failure to resonate with it was a judgement on their own understanding. Consequently the Protestants tended to dismiss the Orthodox, Armenian, and Latin shrines and their rites as superstitious folklore at best, and at worse a conscious fraud perpetrated by the anti-Christ.

The extent of the threat posed by Eastern Christianity to Protestantism was great. The Revd William Jowett felt obliged to quote at length from a Jesuit missionary who wrote that Protestants in the Near East confronted a problem because the rituals of the native Christians were more like Rome and therefore could not be called popish inventions. This Jesuit taunted the Protestants:

> 'It is,' we say to them [the Protestants], 'it is to happy times of Christianity when nascent, that you would have us ascend in order to justify the traditions. It is to the first four centuries, that you appeal on the subject. Ask, then, all these people who surround you [the Eastern Christians]: they will answer, that, in all their practices, (which are the same with ours,) they only follow the Apostolic Traditions – traditions which they received from the famous Antioch, which they regarded as their Mother.' This objection embarrasses our Protestants. They dare not advance that confession, Fasting, Lent,

abstinence, the real presence of Christ in the Eucharist, Purgatory, the Adoration of the Cross, the Invocation of the Saints are Papalistic inventions [*Lettres Edifiantes et Curieuses*, vol. II, p. 167 as quoted in Jowett, p. 25-26].

This attack was seen as sufficiently pointed to deserve a detailed analysis and, of course, rejection.

In the same way the Church of the Holy Sepulchre was almost universally viewed by these Protestants as embodying the worst of the defilements of the Eastern Church and therefore was frequently treated as a threat. The reactions ran the spectrum. Some accepted the site as possibly real, and were even prepared to venerate it as a place sanctified by generations upon generations of believers who worshipped at this spot. But it was not for them where Jesus was to be found.

Notwithstanding the unquestionable poetry of the spot, and the *possibility* of its being the site, or near the site of Christ's sepulchre, it is to us rather impressive as recalling the long ages of pilgrimage which have elapsed since its foundation, than the event of which it claims to be the theatre. We should hardly have supposed, that, under dwellings made with hands, in an atmosphere of superstition and fraud, in the midst of monks, 'black and white, and grey, with all their trumpery', the enlightened Protestant could well be affected, as by the very presence of the awful events of calvary, yet so it is: Mr Wolff says, 'We kneeled down, and I began to pray; but our tears interrupted our words, so we were only able to utter a few broken sentences – we both wept aloud.' For ourselves, we would rather go forth, without the walls, and seek some solitary spot, and endeavor, with the pages of the New Testament before us, in silence to image forth the awful scene. But though we cannot be affected by the Holy Sepulchre, as others may, yet when we think of the thousands who have made this spot the center of their hopes, and in a spirit of piety though not untinctured with superstitious feelings of bygone ages, have endured danger, and toil, and fever, to kneel with bursting hearts upon the sacred rock; then, as regards the history of humanity, we feel it is holy ground [Bartlett, *Walks About Jerusalem*].

This is one of the more charitable observations. Revd W K Tweedie looked at the spot and rejected it outright:

Here [in the Holy Sepulchre] superstition runs riot; here the impulses of emotion are substituted for the power of truth; and here Satan has his seat, – all amid hideous caricatures of the heavenly plan by which the lost are saved [p. 81].

He finds it impossible to accept that this was the place of Jesus' resurrection and is confident that upon further study these places with their 'corrupt, superstitious, blasphemous practice of Christianity . . . will be regarded as mere curiosities' [Tweedie, p. 81].

When the Garden Tomb was proposed as an alternate site of the tomb of Christ, a site where the rocky topography was still intact and where the tomb was similar to the tomb described in the Bible, it became immediately popular among Protestants. There it was possible to 'see' the biblical story coming alive, where no foreign religious element polluted the site with superstitious nonsense. Even today the site is popular among the Evangelical Christians for the same reasons. John Kelman, like many educated Protestant observers, felt the Garden Tomb site was rather dubious but commented on the glorious irony if it were indeed Christ's tomb.

It would indeed be a striking thing, if after all the idolatry of sites which the vision of St. Helena started, the real hill and garden where the world's greatest tragedy was enacted should have gone past Roman and Greek worshippers both, and to have been committed to the hands of the simple Protestants [Kelman, p. 277].

Others were less judicious and, since they wanted it to be true, decided it must be.

The Holy Sepulchre was approached through narrow streets of importuning merchants and insistent beggars. Once inside, the senses were accosted with a virtual carnival atmosphere of pilgrims engaged in extravagant and ostentatious piety – kissing stones and icons, crying profusely, rubbing the stone of unction, and prostrating themselves before the cross on Calvary – all very different from the more regimented piety of their own tradition, where listening to sermons and reciting the liturgy in well orchestrated unison was the norm. Overly demonstrative piety seemed especially jarring to the English Protestant sensibilities. Jowett says of the Holy Sepulchre that although the piety of the people was moving, he could not kneel.

> Our singularity, no doubt, was remarked by them, as we remained standing; but while we have no desire to offend their feelings, we have also no objection to their knowing that Protestants regard these ceremonies, as being vain in the sight of God, and detrimental to the simplicity of the Gospel. I felt, moreover, that it would be difficult for me to rise in this place to the spirit of devotion. The fulsome pageantry of the scene must be first removed: the ground of Mount Calvary, now encumbered with convents, churches, and houses and disguised by splendid altars, gaudy pictures, and questionable reliques, must be cleared, [Jowett, p. 252].

The result was that the Holy Sepulchre came to be viewed as a modern version of the Israelite Temple of Jerusalem. And just as Herod's temple had been taken over by money changers and robbers and had promoted ritualistic sacrifice instead of moral improvement, so the nurturing of these vices were what many pious Protestants perceived in the temple of Jesus resurrection. Their response was that the Temple of Jesus should be cleansed of these inappropriate elements just as Jesus had cleansed the temple in his own day.

Of all the aspects of the Holy Sepulchre which distressed these

Protestant visitors, nothing could compare with the Holy Fire ceremony on the Saturday before Easter. Orthodox, Coptic, Syrian, and Armenian pilgrims with tapers in their hands gathered from all over the world and packed into the church with little or no room to move. In fact many slept in the church Friday night to assure themselves of a prime vantage point for the ceremony. The atmosphere became increasingly excited until a bell announced the patriarch was on his way. Singing and chanting began and local young men (the *shabab*) began shouting and swinging their bodies in a rhythmic movement. Finally into the church snaked the procession and a way would be miraculously cleared among a crowd that seemed to have no slack. The patriarch and Armenian *vartabed* (monk) then disappeared into the sealed tomb, where every light had been extinguished the day before. Shortly from the little round openings in the tomb emerged a hand with a lighted taper. With no visible means of ignition the light was seen as a miraculous sign from God declaring Jesus' resurrection. From person to person the light would travel as the pilgrims lit their own tapers and then passed the light on to family, friend, and strangers alike. Hymns, prayers, and shouts all would intermingle in a cacophony of sounds. Finally the patriarch came out exhausted and would be carried into the Greek Catholicon across from the tomb. The crowd, meanwhile, became even more excited as everyone pushed and shoved to get the light as soon as possible (for that was seen as a favourable sign). The next task was to bring the lighted taper safely home by navigating skilfully through the sea of pilgrims.

It was both the boisterous nature and miraculous claims of the event which so upset the English. Dean Stanley called it "probably the most offensive delusion to be found in the world" [*Sinai and Palestine*, p. 469]. C L Neil's opinion was that it was 'The greatest fraud of all time' [*Rambles in Bible Lands*, p. 134], and Treves said of the Holy Fire: 'it is only to be equalled by those degrading religious orgies which are to be met with in the forests of savage Africa' [p. 77]. He then quoted from Hichen's account of how later on the ceremony degenerates into a kind of witches' sabbath, the church being deafened by frenzied yells and screams, while its floor becomes 'a boiling cauldron filled with arms and hands, with writhing shoulders, backs and knees' [Treves, p. 77].

The Revd Tweedie, whom we have also met already, commented after a brief description of the fire ceremony: 'It seems as if Satan were doing his utmost to stamp out the Truth' [*Jerusalem and Its Environs*, p. 83]. The Church of the Holy Sepulchre and its blasphemous rituals were in need of a thorough cleansing as far as these visitors were concerned.

But since they had neither the influence nor the power to clean out the Holy Sepulchre, these Protestant pilgrims left the Holy Sites to their 'deluded' brothers and sought out instead those places where the spirit of Jesus could still be found. In the landscape and small villages where the biblical stories could be visualized, the Revd William Jowett found a purer inspiration:

> Educated in an early love of Scripture, I cannot describe the emotions excited by beholding the very scene of the most important events recorded in the Old and New Testaments. I have, designedly, kept myself from attending to the traditionary [sic] minutiae which are imposed upon thousands of annual pilgrims. I envy not those who from ignorance and superstitious subjection, are obliged to receive from the lips of hackneyed guides the trifles of Tradition; . . . Good taste and love of truth alike revolt from the details . . . [Jowett, p. 221-222].

A visit to the scenes of the biblical stories is perceived as inspiring, but the sites, with their accumulation of ecclesiastical clutter and puffed-up pedigrees, are best left unattended or visited as a tourist, not a pilgrim.

In the vicinity of Jerusalem, however, was a favourite site which could be visited as both a tourist and a pilgrim – the Mount of Olives.

> It is, I think, the least beautiful hill I can call to mind. [But] this Olivet, this path to the village of Bethany, this way of leading down to the Jordan, are all sacred sites of unquestioned genuineness. This is the country that was

transversed by the feet of Christ. This is the very view that, in every dip and knoll, was familiar to His eyes [Treves p. 86].

Out of the city the landscape could speak with an eloquence that had been drowned out and buried by centuries of misdirected devotion. Later in his book Sir Fredrick Treves opines:

It was in this plain and unassuming country that the religion of Christ was taught. It was taught in the simplest language, in words that a child could understand, and by means of illustrations drawn from the lowliest of subjects. There was in the teaching no stilted ritual, no gorgeous ceremony, no foreshadowing of the princely prelate or the chanting priest. It was a religion associated with such sounds as the splash of a fisherman's net in the lake, the patter of sheep, the call of the shepherd, the tramp of the sower across the fields [p. 87].

This was the pristine Jesus Protestants sought, and it was on Olivet or on the shores of the Sea of Galilee or in the Garden of Gethsemane that this image could best be evoked.

Try as they might to exorcise these places of any inherent holiness, by theological reflections on the spiritual not the material, on the importance of the event not the place, the English pilgrims still could not entirely erase their feelings of holy awe. Canon Bell talks about how 'it does not matter if, after all, we are not able to localize the scenes of the greatest event in the history of the world. It is not the place which is of importance, but the event itself;' [Bell, p. 83]. But he then proceeds to compose a poem on the Garden of Gethsemane, two verses of which are:

It is a place for solemn thought, for solemn thought and prayer,
For bended knee, and humbled heart, head reverently bare;
Here in Gethsemane's dark shade the Savior knelt to pray,
That if it were but possible the cup might pass away.

> Here take thy shoes from off thy feet, for this is holy ground;
> No spot so sacred on this globe from furtherest bound to bound;
> Approach it with a heart subdued, and with a filial fear
> A contrite spirit fitteth all who fain would enter here.
> [Bell, p. 89]

These were places which evoked God, but how and why they had such an effect was frequently avoided because the answer did not fit the Protestant preconceptions.

What theological significance did Jerusalem and the Holy Land have for the Protestants?

The Jesus of the land rather than the sites was of the essence to these Protestant pilgrims, as their accounts and even the titles of their books proclaimed. The 'land' seemed to serve for them two interconnected theological functions. First, it was in a very important and also very Protestant way a sacrament, and second, it was a way of responding to the growing apprehension among the English literary classes that the Bible might not be historically true.

The Holy Land as a sacrament is an idea mentioned by a number of pilgrims, and at first glance it seems an odd designation for these Protestants to use. But it is quickly evident that this is a very Protestant understanding of sacrament. John Kelman writes in his book *The Holy Land*:

> A journey through the Holy Land may reasonably be in some sort a sacramental event in a man's life. Spiritual things are very near us, and we feel that we have a heritage in them; yet they constantly elude us, and need help from the senses to make them real and commanding. Such sacramental help must surely be given by anything that brings vividly to our realization those scenes and that life in the midst of which the Word was made flesh. The more clearly we can gain the impression of places and events in Syria, the more

reasonable and convincing will Christian faith become [Kelman, p. 3].

Later he explicates this thought more closely:

The sacramental quality of the Holy Land is of course felt most by those who seek especially for memoirs and realizations of Jesus Christ. Within the pale of Christianity there are several different ways of regarding the land as holy, and most of them lead to disappointment. The Greek and Roman Catholic churches vie with one another in their passion for sites and relics there, and seem to lose all sense of the distinction between sublime and grotesque in their eagerness for identifications. A Protestant counterpart to this mistaken zeal is that of the huntsman of the fields of prophecy . . . [those who try and read the signs of the end times]. Apart from either of these are others less orthodox but equally superstitious who have some vague notion of occult and magic qualities which differentiate this from other regions of the world . . . It is wiser to abandon the attempt at forcing the supernatural to reveal itself, and to turn to the human side of things as the surest way of ultimately arriving at the divine [Kelman p. 5-6].

The proper understanding of the sacrament, therefore, is to understand its power to bring the Bible and its stories and characters alive, a dramatic way of impressing them more vividly on the memory and the imagination. In this sense the Holy Land was not just illustrative but made Jesus and the Bible real in the same way that Jesus is real in the Lord's Supper – a memory which re-presents Him to those who participate in faith. For most Protestant commentators on the Holy Land, this concept of the relationship to the land is related more to the sacramental theology of Calvin than to that of Zwingli. The re-presentation is more than just a memory (Zwingli); indeed it is a making of Jesus present once again, albeit in a spiritual manner (Calvin).

Another phrase used to express this same idea is that the Holy Land is a fifth gospel or another Bible. J M P Otts, an American but with an attitude very representative of the English Protestants, says of his book:

> This is not a 'book of travels', though it never could have been written if the author had not travelled in Palestine; for it is the result of the careful reading of the Gospels in the lights and shades of the land where Jesus lived and taught. When so read it is found that the land of Jesus so harmonizes with the four written Gospels, and so unfolds and enlarges their meaning, that it forms around them a Fifth Gospel [*The Fifth Gospel: The Land Where Jesus Lived*, p. 5].

Otts drew the term from Renan's use of it in his *Life of Jesus,* but he gave it a very different meaning because, whereas Renan saw the Bible as a human story mistakenly made divine, Otts saw the Bible as a divine story made human and therefore fundamentally sacramental.

Tweedie reiterates the common Protestant theme that the Holy Land can make Jesus come alive in the hearts and imaginations of those who approach in faith:

> A visit to the Land of Promise, so long the land of grief and oppressions, furnishes a thousand proofs and confirmations of the Bible. It is indeed a second Bible, all responsive to the first [Tweedie, p. 102].

To the extent that the Bible stands at the centre of the Protestant faith as the primary vehicle of God's communication to His people, then the Holy Land as a revealer of the Bible and its meaning is itself a form of revelation, making it a channel of grace – a sacrament. Not everyone can travel to the Holy Land, of course, and it is not necessary, in fact, because those who do so can communicate and preserve their experiences (just as the original disciples did) through books about the Holy Land and, eventually, photographic essays. Hence the plethora of Holy Land books produced in English in the nineteenth century. These testimonies allowed others to come to know the Jesus whom the Holy Land proclaims but whose true domain is in the hearts of believers.

These Holy Land books were usually attempts to capture the capacity of the land which had so impressed the traveller, to witness to Jesus and the Bible. Scenery was minutely described and correlated with the appropriate biblical text which it illustrated or vivified. Initially these books might include a few etchings or watercolours, but with the development of photography in the mid-nineteenth century, it became common to supplement the text profusely with pictures. It was only a short time before books like Thompson's *The Land and the Book* appeared which coordinated scenes from the Holy Land and biblical text so that a person could have the edifying effects of a pilgrimage in one's own livingroom. As stereoscopic prints were developed (with the appropriate biblical reference conveniently printed on the card), the realism of this home tour increased. Those pilgrims who actually visited Palestine also wanted to purchase pictures as souvenirs, giving rise to a burgeoning photographic business in Jerusalem. This business began with foreign visitors like Firth, but eventually a native studio was created by Yessayi Garabedian at the Armenian Convent. Later his student, Kirkorian, owned his own studio, and the American Colony (a religious community in Jerusalem) under Eric Matson started taking and selling souvenir photographs, albums, stereoscopes, and postcards to tourists.

At the same time that the ability of the Holy Land to vivify the Bible and make it come imaginatively alive is viewed as sacramental, it is equally important for the Protestants to reject the idea of the Land having any intrinsic merit. The Revd James Cuthbertson waxes poetic on the sites and their moving quality, and then seems obliged to say:

> I pay little attention to what men designate the value of identical places, for the good reason that no merit or moral value can belong to the place per se. The

> stupendous facts of the Death, the Resurrection, and the
> Ascension of Christ being for all times and all ages, their
> influence can be borne in upon the soul as well in one
> country as another. Men are to be saved, not by
> pilgrimages to some distant shrine, not by any human
> efforts – the living, the Divine Christ alone can save from
> sin and future peril [Cuthbertson, p. 61].

Here the doctrine of salvation by grace through faith alone
seems to stand in tension with the Holy Land as a sacrament. The
tension is not truly resolved; rather, as the primacy of faith and the
rejection of the merits of pilgrimage are tagged onto a description
of the powerful nature of the Holy Land experience. This was the
common solution.

The second theological function which the Holy Land served
for Protestant pilgrims was to give renewed credence to the Bible as
it came under attack from the corrosive effects of historical and
scientific criticism. The majority of those visiting the Holy Land as
faithful pilgrims were vague about the nature of the criticism being
levelled against the Bible. It was not a specific intellectual problem
or set of problems that concerned them, but rather an uneasiness
that old assumptions no longer stood so confidently against the
powers of unbelief. Living as they did in the midst of a century
where the 'Bible story' was being dissected into a whole host of
different and often contending sources, they felt their religious
foundations shake as the *Zeitgeist* or the March of Mind seemed to
threaten the Bible as the Word of God. In the increasingly
industrialized, secularized and scientized West, the Bible seemed to
be losing its credibility. It spoke of miracles, it drew upon exotic and
quaint characters and customs. The Bible was becoming
increasingly marginalized from real life. To these people the Holy
Land seemed to provide 'evidence' of the truth of the Bible because,
if 'read' properly, the topography, the geography, and the customs of
the area seemed to make the Bible sensible and therefore credible
once again. It was not a specific response to specific attacks but
provided a generalized feeling of renewed confidence, because the
imagery, customs, and atmosphere of the Bible meshed so

thoroughly with the Holy Land. This was particularly welcomed by those who did not want to accept the sanitized, demythologized Bible being created in Western universities.

This argument that the Holy Land is an 'evidence' for the truth of the Bible and therefore Christianity is well framed by Otts in his *Fifth Gospel: The Land Where Jesus Lived*.

> Thus the well-informed and observant traveler in the land of the Bible will find more to confirm its truth and unfold its meaning while journeying through the land where Jesus lived, than he could ever gather from whole acres of printed evidences of Christianity [p. 31].

Yet this evidence for the truth of the Bible, unlike the evidential theology developed by John Locke, is not based upon logical argument but upon the persuasiveness of the experience of the Holy Land in relationship to the Bible story and the resonance created by the juxtaposition of the two. In this way it is part of the shedding of the Enlightenment's search for logical evidence and a turn to the more Romantic concern with experiential persuasion.

A minority of the pilgrims were aware of the intricacies surrounding the discussion on the nature of the Bible and the type of truth it meant to convey. They had read Strauss' and Renan's *Life of Jesus*, they had read or read about the ideas of biblical interpretation promulgated in *Essays and Reviews*. For these people the collapse, prompted by historical criticism, of the Jesus Christ of tradition, the Jesus of divine power (miracles) and prerogative (judge), challenged them to return to the Jesus of Galilee, the man who stood behind the myth created by nineteen hundred years of obfuscating tradition. Owen Chadwick comments on these well-informed, up-to-date believers in *The Secularization of the European Mind*:

> For some religious men of the middle nineteenth century the 'discovery' of the historical Jesus gave a marvellous fresh food for their faith. They had known, or had hardly known, a remote figure of ritual, and now

> perceived the humanity at last. They felt they could
> begin where the apostles began – come to a man because
> he was such a man, and then slowly find conviction that
> more was in him than man [Chadwick, p. 226].

Well, what better place to begin this search for the 'historical'
Jesus than in the Land of Jesus – this same sentiment we have already
seen expressed by Kelman: 'It is wiser to abandon the attempt at
forcing the supernatural to reveal itself, and to turn to the human
side of things as the surest way of ultimately arriving at the divine'
[Kelman p. 3]. The Holy Land was, therefore, for some a way not
only to get behind the Jesus of the Church but also to get behind
the Jesus of the Bible to the historical Jesus and confront him
personally (as the disciples did), and out of this personal relationship
rediscover the Jesus of faith.

For those who sought not to reaffirm the complete inerrancy of
the Bible nor to find the historical Jesus behind the Christ of the
gospels, there was the reasonable interaction between geography and
Bible which, like the symbiotic relationship between history and the
Bible, and science and the Bible, could deepen the faith rather than
destroy it. Dean Stanley, the famous biographer of Thomas Arnold,
was such a personage. A leading figure of the Broad Church faction
he argued in his preface to *Sinai and Palestine* that although the
significance of the geography of the Holy Land is easy to exaggerate,
its relationship to the Sacred History is, if properly used, a fruitful
one. He goes on to enumerate six specific ways that the connection
can be helpfully employed.

In all cultures history is influenced by geography, so the
geography of the Holy Land helps explain the biblical culture and
therefore the Bible itself. Second, the geography is bound to effect
the images which a culture's poets and philosophers will use, so
knowing the land will be useful in elucidating their thought. One
example is the new appreciation experientially gained of such
passages as 'The shadow of a great rock in a weary land' [Isaiah 22:2]
after having to seek the cool shade, even of a rock, in the boiling
heat of Palestine [Cuthbertson, p. 129]. Third, the geography can be
used to explain specific actions, such as why Jesus went to certain

towns (the road network) or why battles were conducted in certain ways (the topography of the battlefield). Fourth, the coincidence of biblical narrative and geography provides a presumption or evidence of its fundamental truthfulness.

> It is impossible not to be struck by the constant agreement between recorded history and the natural geography both of the Old and New Testament. To find a marked correspondence between the scenes of the Sinaitic mountains and the events of the Israelite wanderings is not much perhaps, but it is certainly something towards a proof of the truth of the whole narrative. To meet Gospel allusions, transient but yet precise, to the localities of their early origin . . . Such coincidences are not usually found in fables of Eastern origin [p. xix-xx].

Fifth, beyond the real connection between the Bible and the Land rests the ability of the places, especially the landscape, to vivify the biblical story because 'the framework of life, of customs, of manners, even of dress and speech, is still substantially the same as it was ages ago' [p. xxiv]. Finally, 'the whole journey, as it is usually taken by modern travellers, presents the course of history as a living parable before us, to which no other journey or pilgrimage can present any parallel' [p. xxvi]. Here he means that a pilgrimage allows the Bible to be seen as a sacred history or drama rather than a set of proof texts – a holy history where God is not the history itself but is revealed through it. This approach accorded with that which Thomas Arnold took to the Old Testament. For Stanley the ability of the Holy Land to re-present the Bible stories (the sacramental), and the evidential nature of the coincidence of land and text, combined with other factors to underline the value of a pilgrimage for English Protestants. So these six factors collectively gave the Holy Land a special appeal and provided an argument for Christianity's truth, a position reinforced during his second visit when he accompanied the Prince of Wales to the Holy Sites.

Besides the theological significance of the Holy Land, it was also seen as witnessing to the superiority of Western culture and the Protestant religion. Almost all the English commentators who wrote about the Holy Land in the nineteenth century saw it as a land which was cursed. The physical manifestation of this curse was seen in the desolation of the land, especially in the decay of a once fertile land into scrub and desert, and in the diseased populace, suffering not just from physical disease but from economic, political, and spiritual disease as well. The reason for this curse was again almost universally identified with the consequences of rejecting the overtures of God.

> The incompleteness of Syria [Holy Land] – the thing in which her life has been most lamentably unfinished – was her response to the revelation of her God. She never was at pains to understand it; she never fully opened her heart to its new progress, nor felt her high destiny as the bearer of good tidings to the world. She never seriously set herself to obey its plainest ethical demands. The wreckage is her price paid for the neglect. No man nor nation can finish any task to perfection, who has not done justice to such revelation of God as his heart and conscience have received . . . Right dealing with revelation is the secret of all efficient performance [Kelman, p. 203].

The rejection of Jesus and God's condemnation of Israel, leading to the destruction of the Temple and the exile of the Jews, reinforced by the Islamic conquests, were all interpreted as bringing about a curse on the land and its people. And so the 'Land of Milk and Honey' was transformed into the land of death.

> Never was symbolism more appropriate than that of the Holy Fire in the Church of the Holy Sepulchre. The very heart and soul of [the Holy Land] is a tomb – the reputed grave of Jesus Christ. To this day the chief pilgrim song repeats with exultant reiteration the words, 'This is the Tomb of Christ.' . . . It is not, however, the

victory over death that impresses one as the spirit of [the Holy Land]. It is death itself, unconquered, mysterious, and dark [Kelman, p. 228-9].

This theme of a land cursed because it has rejected God's revelation was supported by comparing the cities of Hebron and Bethlehem. The first was an Islamic town and as such, despite an outward appearance of thriving fields, a place as 'stagnant as a deserted pond . . . It is moribund with a vengeance! The sullenness of people you meet on the road give a token of its spirit before you enter . . . Women draw aside their veils to curse us as we passed. Stones flung by unseen hands behind walls' [Kelman, p. 233]. Bethlehem was a different story. As Conder commented in *Tent Works,* 'Christian villages thrive and grow, while the Moslem ones fall into decay' [p. 314]. Bethlehem represented 'the contrast between Christianity and Islam, between the vitality of the religion of progress and civilization, and the hopeless stagnation of a fatalistic creed [p. 314]. Often, as these extracts show, the characteristics that breed sloth and dishonesty were seen as being encouraged by Islam, especially the idea of fatalism.

With the theme of the 'cursed land', the theological concern with evidences for the truth of Christianity, and by extension the falsity of Judaism and Islam, begins to transform into a more overtly political concern. It is not merely that the condition of Palestine shows its denial of God, but that to turn to pure Christianity – that is, English Protestantism – can mean a revival of the land. The theological point becomes an imperialistic one.

What was the Protestant Political Agenda?

As the English visitors compared Palestine under the Turks with those parts of the Orient which they controlled, especially Egypt, they felt they had sufficient evidence that British rule brought not only economic prosperity but 'freedom' to the native populations – that is, freedom from the political tyranny of the Ottoman empire and its rapacious taxes, freedom from the caprice of local a governor, freedom from a corrupt bureaucracy, freedom from an enslaved judiciary, and cultural freedom for the persecuted minorities, especially Jews and Christians. For many English pilgrims the foundation of their own society, with its obvious political, economic, and moral success, and therefore the instrument for lifting the curse from Palestine, was the Protestant Church. It was hoped and expected that the Protestant Church of England, through its mission churches, hospitals, and schools, would change the face of Palestine. This would be accomplished by educating the next generation in Western (Protestant) political, social, and religious values. Once the native population had been culturally 'converted', the next step would be obvious – British rule. Bishop Hannington during his visit in 1884 stopped at a Druse village with an English mission school. There he was told by the local sheiks that "the topic which is nearest to their hearts is English occupation" in order to drive out the Turks and bring real civilization. Kelman also saw the introduction of Western technology, such as the telegraph and railroads along with the expansion of trade and tourism and economic prosperity, as essential but warned that the real salvation of Palestine would reside not in technology but in faith.

> Interesting and important as all this advance of Western progress is, it is not from it that the resurrection of the Holy Land must be expected. There, as elsewhere, the chief danger of the present time is that of godless civilization, whose purely secular and materialistic prosperity may prove to be more of a curse than a blessing after all [Kelman, p. 290].

So the real hope of Palestine lay in its religious conversion to the Protestant faith, from which all sorts of material blessings as well as spiritual ones would flow. Then the landscape itself would be transformed. Where there were deserts and deserted villages, trees and crops would grow again and the land, like the people, would be redeemed. Eustace Martin, a pilgrim who published his *Visit to the Holy Land, Syria and Constantinople* in 1883, summed up this attitude:

> The whole legislative wisdom of the British people is, I believe, in every land honoured, the activity of commerce, their respect for and support of public order, the sense of duty which is insensible to danger, their civil and religious freedom, their enterprise and industry; I believe that all those qualities and natural characteristics have sprung from and been developed by the teaching of the Bible. It is the great book of reform [Martin, p. 104].

Reform in religion would therefore lead to reform in social, political, and economic conditions, and that in turn would redeem the land.

This quasi-messianic role for Britain had a great deal to do with the willingness of the British to exert time and energy to bring about the 'liberation' of Palestine during World War I, and later their fascination with their role as occupiers. The idea that with religious and political redemption the land would return to a fruitful and forested state also helps explain the West's glorification of Israel's re-forestation and making the desert bloom projects. Here the nineteenth century ideal of redeeming the fallen Holy Land was being realized, even if by the very people whose denial of Jesus was blamed for its decline into misery. But by then, for many people, the line between religion and culture was not very clear. As the imperialism of Christianity waned with the expansion of secularism, the imperialism of Western culture continued unabated.

What significance did the Holy Land have for these English Protestant pilgrims? It was, as we have seen, a complex combination of religious sacramentalism, proof for the validity of the Bible, and affirmation of their religious, social, and moral superiority.

Russian Orthodox Pilgrims

Who were they?

T he majority of Russian pilgrims belonged to a very different socio-economic class than their English counterparts. Most of them were poverty-stricken, illiterate peasants. The statistics kept by the various Russian societies promoting pilgrimage indicate that peasants made up between 80 to 90 percent of Russians visiting the Holy Land. Of the 10,000 or more pilgrims recorded between 1882 and 1889, over 8,000 were classed as peasants; a further 323 were ecclesiastics of one sort or another. Of the remaining pilgrims, 1,227 were categorized as government officials of various levels of importance, 270 were from the nobility, and only 169 from the mercantile class. These same proportions are present in later tabulations as well, although the overall numbers rise considerably. In the five years from 1895 to 1899, 26,104 Russian pilgrims were registered, and in 1900 alone 6,000 Russians, most during Easter, appeared in Jerusalem. Not only does the percentage of peasants remain very high, but there is also a consistent ratio of around 60 percent women to 40 percent men [Stavrou, p. 150].

The other major difference between the Russians and the English pilgrim was age. While there were some notable elderly travellers from England, most were in middle-age or younger and in somewhat robust health. The Russians, on the other hand, were predominantly elderly, and many were in such poor health that they died during the pilgrimage, which was viewed by their compatriots as a somewhat enviable way to enter the afterlife.

One Western observer, the Revd Andrew Gray, describes his exposure to the Russians during a 1903 pilgrimage:

> The road was crowded with Russian pilgrims, most of them past middle life, and quite as many women as men, who had walked from their homes in the interior of their distant land, to the nearest seaport, whence they might reach the confines of the Holy Land, to begin anew their pilgrimage on foot to the sacred places. These pilgrims bore with them their necessary equipments of travel. Most of them (women as well as men) trudged along with a stout stick, evidently intent only on what they were doing, and hardly looking at their right hand or their left in their march to the place where their Lord and master was born. Among the younger women were a few with the Madonna type face – sweet, serious, and intensely devotional. There were lads with simple, good-natured faces, but lacking the keen activity and intellectual expression of youth of like age with us. The old men, with their wrinkled, frosty, and yet kindly faces, moved on as alert as the youngest. we saw these pilgrims at every shrine or sepulchre we visited [Gray, p. 44].

This peasant army of Russians almost occupied the Holy Places during Easter.

Because of the illiteracy of these Russian peasants, there is not a large body of literature which we can draw upon to recount their experiences, expectations, and exasperation. Stephen Graham, the Anglo-Russian who wrote a moving and detailed account in his book *With the Russian Pilgrims to Jerusalem*, commented that the peasant pilgrims could not compose a literary account of their journey, while those Russians who could were so removed from and dismissive of the culture and beliefs of the peasants as to be unable or unwilling to do so. Therefore, the Russian experience will rely upon the evidence, much of it statistical, of the Russian Orthodox Palestine Society and its predecessor, the Palestine Committee, and of Western observers of varying degrees of knowledge and accuracy.

Why do they visit the Holy Land?

The simple answer for most Russian peasants journeying to Jerusalem to the question, 'why did they want to go?' would be: in order to prepare for death. Exactly what the connection was might be rather vague, but it would be seen by most as an appropriate response. Graham related a passage from *The Brothers Karamazov* where Dostoevsky speaks of the peasant contemplative who hoards up images and then one day begins to act upon them. To someone who saw only the immediate circumstances, those actions would seem sudden and irrational, but behind the scenes much had gone into creating the response, which had its own logic and meaning. Likewise with deciding to go on a pilgrimage to the Holy Land; much contributed to create the desire [Graham, p. 88-89].

If the primary motivating factor for the Protestants was the Bible, and the desire to have it vivified and verified, then the Russian equivalent was the divine liturgy and the icons. The divine liturgy is filled with imagery of the Holy Land and talks about the altar as the tomb from which comes the healing power of Christ to overcome death. Gregory Palamas connects the liturgy and the Sepulchre:

> the house of God here is a true symbol of that tomb . . .
> For behind the curtain it has the room in which the body
> will be laid and there too the holy altar. Whoever
> therefore hastens to draw near to the divine mystery and
> the place where it is, and who perseveres to the end . . .
> will without doubt see the Lord . . . [Wybrew, p. 152].

If every divine liturgy is a re-enactment of the passion in Jerusalem and every altar the tomb of Christ and every church a Holy Sepulchre, why not go to the archetype, that very tomb where Jesus' body was buried and from which He arose? The tomb in Jerusalem was called the Life-Giving Tomb by the Russians because it was here that Christ conquered death, and although every altar was the tomb and every church Jerusalem, still the idea persisted that in the earthly Jerusalem the heavenly Jerusalem was more intensely and clearly mirrored.

The icons also inspired Russians to visit the Holy Land because it was so frequently the backdrop to the sacred scenes portrayed. A quick survey of significant Russian icons for the various seasons demonstrates, for example, the baptism of Jesus at the Jordan River, the nativity in the manger in Bethlehem, the Transfiguration on Mt Tabor, and the crucifixion in Jerusalem. As the theology of icons made them windows into the sacred realities which they pictured and a source of divine energy, so the Holy Land must be in some way an icon of that which took place there and a valuable window into the sacred mystery of Christ's birth, life, death, and resurrection [Lossky, *The Mystical Theology of the Eastern Church*, p. 189].

People differed as to the particular ways that the imagery of the liturgy and the icons shaped their desire to visit the Holy Land, under the influence of Orthodox ideas of grace, sacraments, penance, and the quest for union with God (the ultimate pilgrimage), but they universally agreed upon the efficacy of going. This belief was reinforced, of course, by those pilgrims who returned and recounted stories of the wonders they had seen. Graham tells of one pilgrim, Abraham, who journeyed to Jerusalem every year. When asked how he had become interested in the Holy Land, Abraham related that the stories told by pilgrims staying at his home had so mesmerized and moved him that at age seven he had hidden away crusts of bread and, once well supplied, had taken off. When questioned by a waggoner where he was going, he replied Jerusalem. He was told to hop on and the wagon would take him there. He fell asleep, he awoke and asked where they were, the driver answered, Jerusalem. Getting off the wagon, he was confronted by his mother – he had been driven home [Graham, p. 249-50].

But home was really never anywhere except the heavenly Jerusalem, so Abraham's life was spent travelling from Russia to Jerusalem and back until the day when the journey of life was over and the true Jerusalem attained. Abraham was a symbol of the

Russian pilgrimage as a whole. To go to the Holy Land on pilgrimage was seen as a vicarious visit to one's future home – the heavenly Jerusalem – and it was also an act of penance and prayer by means of which one obtained the grace to ensure one arrived. It was not only a foretaste of heaven but also a ticket to the celestial Jerusalem. The souvenirs, the blessings, the vicarious identifications with Christ's sufferings (through suffering oneself and visiting the places of Jesus' suffering), the burial shroud dipped in the Jordan, the ceremonies at the shrines and especially the Holy Week rites – all these were symbols of Christ's victory over death and promises of the same to all who believed in Him and shared His baptism. And they were not just symbols, but *effectual* symbols, symbols that like the icons put one in touch with the reality they represented. So the pilgrims went to Jerusalem to prepare for death and by doing so expected to inherit eternal life.

Because it was a preparation for death, most pilgrims went at the end of life after their working life was finished. The family was raised, the work in the fields was in younger hands, and now thoughts could turn to Jerusalem. The family, the village (*mir*), the Tsar had all been satisfied, and it was time to attend to God. As life began to shorten, the focus was less on the earthly village than on the heavenly one, where all would be united in community (*mir*) and peace (*mir*) – the New Jerusalem! It was also customary for those who had partaken in the pilgrimage to Jerusalem to lead a celibate life on their return, and it was thought to be easier for the elderly to follow this aspect of the tradition. [Bishop Theophanus, Superior of Bethlehem, related this to us in one of our many enlightening discussions.]

Throughout history the Russian peasants had travelled to Jerusalem, usually walking the whole way. What changed in the nineteenth century was the development of 'cheap' mass transport and a governmental policy to encourage pilgrimage. An unprecedented number of peasants took advantage of the desire to visit and possibly die in Jerusalem. Why this governmental interest is itself an interesting question. Various governmental missions and private societies under royal patronage were created during the nineteenth century to promote Russian interests in the Holy Land, but often they had conflicting aims. The foreign ministry was frequently interested in developing a Russian presence and influence in the Ottoman empire. The growing number of pilgrims and Russia's role as protector of the Arab Orthodox population provided ample justification for involvement, a pretext for interference in the affairs of the empire. But as it was also occasionally politic to support the sultan, the government sometimes moved to restrain the more active Russian expansionist elements.

For a number of reasons the Church itself had a difficult time developing a coherent strategy towards the Holy Land. The control of the state over the Holy Synod meant that often the interests of the Church were not expressed in the Church's own policy. Also there were complications working with the Orthodox Patriarch of Jerusalem, who was Greek. The Greek Patriarch was not always sympathetic to the Russian agenda, but there were political, theological, and practical difficulties operating without or against him because he technically had jurisdiction over his Russian co-religionists. Some churchmen wanted to co-opt the Greek presence, especially because they were doing so little for the Arab-speaking Orthodox population. Others wanted to co-operate and develop a strong Orthodox presence in the face of Roman Catholic and Protestant gains of both converts and a visible institutional presence (churches, hospitals, and schools) in Jerusalem. These various strands all contended for power and influence over the various Russian institutions in the Holy Land, and this conflict ultimately diminished the Russian role.

The one area where agreement was fairly consistent was over the need to build pilgrim hostels, hospitals and support services. This infrastructure, with the favourable transportation arrangements mentioned earlier, made the large number of pilgrims possible and meant they were well catered for when they arrived. Food, shelter, water, tours, banking, and spiritual guidance were all provided.

But if the government and other interest groups made it financially and physically feasible to make a pilgrimage, it was still the desire of the peasants to visit the Life-Giving Tomb and thereby prepare for a life-giving death which motivated them to go.

Plate 1   *Wooden barracks accommodation in the Russian Compound for the Russian peasant pilgrims*

Plate 2   *Russian pilgrims attending an open air mass on the banks of Lake Tiberius*

Plate 3   *Russian pilgrims arriving at their encampment on the River Jordan*

Plate 4   *Russian pilgrims setting out on a day's excursion to the Holy Places. They are escorted by a Bedouin horseman (right) and a Montenegran* kawass *(dragoman) of the Russian Church (left)*

Plate 5   *Orthodox pilgrims attend Maundy Thursday washing of the feet morning service in the parvis of the Holy Sepulchre. The Greek Orthodox patriarch officiates from the raised platform*

Plate 6   *Throngs of pilgrims crowding every nook and cranny of the parvis of the Holy Sepulchre during Easter Week celebrations*

Plate 7   *Russian pilgrims leaving the Church of the Resurrection with palms in their hands*

Plate 8   *Russian pilgrims bathe with their white shrouds in the holy waters of the Jordan River. It was considered a great honour to be buried with shrouds sanctified in the river where Christ himself was baptized*

Plate 9   *Bethlehem residents in their traditional costumes intermingled with pilgrims awaiting the arrival of the Christmas procession in Manger Square*

Plate 10   *In 1894 clergyman, Bishop Vincent, usually a critic of Orthodox piety, annotated the above photo, '. . . Before us [is] a recess where fifteen lamps are suspended, six belonging to the Greeks, five to the Armenians and four to the Latins. And in the floor of a recess a silver star is placed in the pavement of which are these words: Hic de Virginie Maria Jesus Christus Natus est. Here let all prejudices for the moment vanish, and let us observe the reverent manner of the worshippers. Whatever else they believe in they believe in Christ, the Babe, the Man, the Deity incarnate.'*

Plate 11   Pilgrim Greek clergy holding crosses in front of the Holy Sepulchre

Plate 12   *Protestant American pilgrims on the outskirts of Jerusalem, leaving for an excursion accompanied by local escorts*

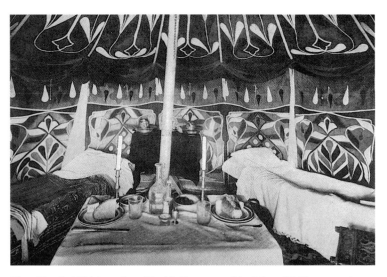

Plate 13   *In 1894 the author of* Earthly Footsteps of the Man of Galilee *wrote about his photo, 'Travellers now ride on English saddles and on excellent horses, sleeping at night in carpeted tents most comfortably furnished.'*

Plate 14   *'Inside the Garden of Gethsemane the Eastern churches have placed ... the "stations" representing the various incidents of the crucifixion. We [Protestant pilgrims] were here during the Greek Easter week, and many pilgrims were making the rounds of the "stations" in the garden.' Note the city walls and the Golden Gate in the background*

Plate 15 *Special pilgrim boats sailing out to pick up pilgrims from the ships anchored beyond the forbidding rocks of Jaffa harbour. Note the name Rolla Floyd on the bow. Floyd was one of the most popular dragomen for English and American pilgrims and tourists*

Plate 16 *Russian pilgrims resting on the way to the Jordan River.*

Plate 17   *Protestant pilgrims on the banks of the Jordan River*

Plate 18   *Encampment of Protestant pilgrims*

Plate 19   *This photo entitled, 'The Lord is my Shepherd', from the Twenty Third Psalm series of the American Colony studio in Jerusalem beautifully depicts how the Protestant pilgrim wanted to experience the Holy Land – a Palestine untouched by the passage of almost two millennia*

Plate 20 *The oak at Mamre was a favourite site for the Russian pilgrim who knew the story of Abraham and his three holy guests from some of the most well-loved Orthodox icons*

Plate 21 *A bit of the Holy Fire safely housed in a lantern for its journey to Mother Russia*

Plate 22 *Russian pilgrims with their banners on their way to the Jordan River*

Plate 23   *A Russian pilgrim triumphantly dries his shroud on a cane cut from a bush along the bank of the Jordan River*

Plate 24   *Local inhabitants pose outside of the site tradition sanctions as the tomb of Lazarus. Although they remarked that this site was 'but a tradition', Protestant pilgrims believed 'the strong possibility … that the tomb is not very far away'*

Plate 25 *The entrance into the Life-Giving Tomb within the Church of the Resurrection (Holy Sepulchre). This is the enhanced glorified tomb so familiar to Russian Pilgrims from their icons*

Plate 26 *'The tomb of our Lord, "The New Calvary". outside of Jerusalem.' This is Gordon's tomb outside of Damascus gate accepted by some Protestants as the more probable site of Christ's entombment in accord with their desire to discover the authentic unembellished Redeemer. (Note the photographer's addition of the two women to intensify the identification with the gospel account.)*

What did the Russians do when they came to the Holy Land?

The itinerary and activities of the Russian pilgrims were much more communal and determined than those of the independent Protestants (with the exception of those Protestants on an organized tour), but within the structure there existed a great deal of freedom. It was a bit like an Orthodox service in which there is one major event, the liturgy, but people are all milling around visiting the icons and engaged in their own devotions. And, just as in the service, the spirit is communal despite the lack of orchestration and common activity. For most Russians the pilgrimage began not in Jaffa but at home, where they began preparing for the trip by hoarding away old crusts of bread which they used as their staple food on the journey. This bread, when put in water after the mold had been scrapped off, could give nourishment in the form of a soup or bread pudding. The pilgrim also collected money from friends and fellow villagers to purchase holy souvenirs or to make donations to the monks in the Holy Land, who then prayed for the souls of the pilgrim's loved ones. The pilgrimage itself commenced with the act of leaving home, and many walked to a seaport. stopping at shrines along the way and sleeping rough or as the honoured guest of some peasants, who deemed sheltering pilgrims a source of blessing. For those who did not fancy the more penitential walk, there were inexpensive train fares available for pilgrims, or one could ride as a 'hare'. This latter category required the pilgrim to squat rabbit-like under a seat in the train for the journey.

One of the policies of the government was to encourage a domestic steamship industry to challenge the position of the Austrians' Lloyds. So most pilgrims travelled on Russian ships packed with passengers on deck and in empty holds. The atmosphere on these ships was tatty and pungent, but also strangely calm. Virtually everyone had decided to forgo alcohol until the Easter feast, and so, despite close quarters, the tone was sedate and even religious, with groups praying together and singing hymns. Wherever the ship put into port, a collection of pilgrims would set out to visit any local shrines.

Arriving at Jaffa, they were met by representatives of the Russian Orthodox Palestine Society, who would escort them to the Greek monastery where the floor of one wing was spread with straw pallets. Once the railroad to Jerusalem was built in 1892, the pilgrim had to decide which route to take – the more comfortable and more expensive train or the cheaper, gruelling but more appropriately penitential trip by foot. Whether by train or foot, the pilgrims travelled together and were met again by a Society dragoman, usually a physically imposing Montenegrin, and escorted to the hostels within the Russian compound. The compound, built in 1864 outside the city walls and centred on the multi-domed cathedral, provided both a material symbol of Russia's presence and a place to minister to the needs of pilgrims.

The new arrivals at the hostel in Jerusalem were welcomed by those already there like long-lost loved ones. 'It gave me the idea that after death, when, after life's pilgrimage the Russians come to the judgement seat, there will be such a feeling of brotherhood and affection . . . ' [Graham, p. 85]. Those already resident served as initiators into the customs of the place and acted as guides to the city for those who had just come. It was the policy of the hostel to take a deposit of money from each pilgrim as they arrived, so that if they were robbed by bandits or unscrupulous merchants, there would be something left for the homeward journey. The hostel also served as a bank to safeguard their money, although few peasants seemed to trust any official with their coins.

The Society's tickets were round trip and good for a year, but those who came to Jerusalem for one feast were expected to leave before the next began. There were four major pilgrim feasts during the year. Easter was the most momentous; the others were Ascension Day, the Assumption of the Virgin, and Christmas. The feast around which the pilgrimage centred provided the major focus for the pilgrims' activities, but other sites and experiences were sought as well.

The Easter pilgrimage attracted three-fourths of the year's visitors, partially because of the favourable weather but primarily because the celebration of Christ's victory over death was the central message of the Church and the major concern of the pilgrim. The

Easter pilgrimage centred around the Holy Week events, but there were also a number of other edifying excursions. There was a long and arduous journey to Nazareth and the Sea of Galilee, stopping at Mt Tabor, of Transfiguration fame, en route. This trip took four days each way; the pilgrims tried to be in Nazareth for the feast of the Annunciation on 25 March if Easter were not too close and they could get back to Jerusalem for Holy Week. The pilgrims returning from this journey were met on the outskirts of Jerusalem and accompanied back to the Russian Compound with such joy that many Western observers felt that these were people just arriving from Russia by foot. Their bedraggled appearance would reinforce such a misapprehension.

There was also a mandatory trip to Bethlehem to visit the manger and a stop at the tree of Mamre, where Abraham lived and gave hospitality to the three angels. In Orthodox iconography Mamre represents both the Trinity and the foretelling of the eucharistic meal, so it was popular with the Russian pilgrims, who eventually bought it as a Holy Site. The most important excursion, however, was to the Jordan River. As part of the preparation for Holy Week, it was traditional for the pilgrims to walk to Jericho, where they spent the night and then continued on the next day to the spot of Jesus' baptism, an oasis of trees and flowers symbolizing the spiritual fertility of the acts performed there. Before leaving Jerusalem each person would buy one or more burial shrouds to wear as they went into the river in a rite of symbolic baptism. Thousands lined up on the river bank wearing their white shrouds while the priest blessed the water by dipping crosses into the flowing stream. Once the preliminaries were over, they jumped, slipped, or slowly lowered themselves into the water, re-enacting their being entombed with Christ so that later, when present at His resurrection in Jerusalem, they could participate in His victory over death. It all symbolized Paul's assertion that those who are baptized into Christ's death will share His resurrection, but like all Orthodox rites it was not a mere remembrance but an effectual, sacramental symbol which conveyed what it represented.

Once the religious component of the visit was satisfied, there was a festive atmosphere which permeated the proceedings. In

1883, while camped with a Cook's Tour, Canon Bell observed:

> Some of the men dashed naked into the stream to exhibit
> their prowess; and some swam races in the rapid stream . . .
> while the more devout among the bathers will often join
> hands in the water, and recite the creed, dipping their
> heads in the water after each sentence, and holding on to
> the branches of the trees that bend above the banks [Bell,
> p. 113].

Everyone seemed to enjoy the experience in their own way but
without losing the central baptismal theme. Once the people had
bathed, been blessed and had some fun, they emerged from the
water and sat in rows along the bank drying out and filling small
water bottles to bring home.

Eventually, with their shrouds hung on sticks like flags, the
pilgrims meandered down to the Dead Sea to view the place which
tradition marked out as the location of the Last Judgement. The
priests would provide commentary along the way, pointing out how
the river of life sank into the lake of death to symbolize the fall of
humanity. The imagery reiterated the human need to be lifted up
out of the curse of death by the Life-Giving Tomb of Christ back in
Jerusalem, to which the pilgrims now slowly returned, stopping at a
monastery or two on the way.

For the Russian pilgrim each of these excursions represented an
important divine mystery. Bethlehem was, of course, the place of
the Incarnation. Further to the south was Mamre, where the
doctrine of the mystery of the Trinity was prefigured in the angelic
triumvirate who visited Abraham. (One of the finest and most
famous of all Orthodox icons, the Holy Trinity painted by Rublev,
depicts the three angelic visitors in solemn splendour as they partake
of Abraham's hospitality.) The life and teachings of Jesus were
especially celebrated in Nazareth and the Sea of Galilee. 'Here He
pronounced great truths, here were accomplished most of His
miracles, almost the whole gospel was fulfilled on the shores of the
Sea of Galilee' [Khitrof, as quoted in Graham, p. 212]. Finally the
Jordan River, the place of Christ's baptism, was symbolic of the

entry of the faithful into the soteriological work of Jesus, which in turn made the Dead Sea, representing death and judgement, something which could be faced without fear. By visiting each of these places in turn, the pilgrim not only followed the life of Christ but meditated upon the divine mysteries embedded in each event.

The central feature of every pilgrimage, however (especially of the Easter one), was the Holy and Life-Giving Tomb of Christ in Jerusalem. The Holy Sepulchre, with its village of chapels commemorating various elements of Christ's passion, was primarily home of the two major sites of Christendom: the hill of Golgotha and the Tomb itself. Every pilgrim visited the Church, but in Holy Week the rites and the place coincided. Graham's description compared the Russian pilgrims during that Holy Week to a lamp before a shrine because they seemed never to sleep and always were prostrate before a holy site.

The Holy Week services began for the pilgrims on Lazarus Saturday the day before Palm Sunday when they gathered in Bethany, site of Lazarus' resurrection, to march into Jerusalem, picking flowers and waving palms bought from Arab merchants. The occasion was a festive one, with stops at various churches along the way and devotions at Bithsphania, where the ass's colt used by Jesus was collected by the apostles. A large number went out the night before and slept there in order to be ready for the procession. The event ended with a grand service at the Holy Sepulchre conducted by the patriarch and accompanying bishops and monks in glamorous vestments.

> The new crystal lamps were lit, and innumerable wax candles; the black depth of the church was agleam with lights like a starlit sky brought down from heaven. The singing was glorious [Graham, p. 241-42].

The Palm Sunday service the next morning was equally impressive, using a large olive tree decked out with flowers in a three-fold procession around the Sepulchre. At the end of the service this tree was cut into bits and distributed to the pilgrims, who would cherish it as a relic and take it home in great honour [Graham, p. 243].

On the Monday of Holy Week those pilgrims who had not yet visited the Jordan and prepared for their Easter communion did so. Wednesday many went to the monastery of St Constantine and St Helena to watch the consecration of holy oil.

Holy Thursday services began an almost twenty-four hour a day regimen for the dedicated pilgrim. On Thursday morning the patriarch performed the Washing the Feet service in the courtyard of the Holy Sepulchre Church. This act of humility came dear to those who watched because they were charged for the privilege. Later that day the patriarch took a service at the Sepulchre commemorating Christ's sufferings; the gospels were read in a multitude of languages. Most Russians, however, would return to the Russian Cathedral in the Russian Compound for their communion, preferring the Russian language service. Now the white loaves of bread were blessed which would be returned to them the next day. This bread was then to be taken home as a special treasure to be shared with loved ones [Graham, p. 276].

Good Friday commenced with the service of Great Hours at 9.00am and High Vespers at 2.00pm. At this time most pilgrims began to take up their places in the Holy Sepulchre, which they guarded tenaciously until the Holy Fire Saturday afternoon. For this long vigil they brought along stools and a small food supply. At 8.30pm on Friday evening the procession and burial of the Holy Shroud would take place. Two by two the participants would appear before the patriarch for his blessing, put on their robes and, when all was ready, march to Golgotha. There, on a table, would be a shroud with the embroidered picture of Jesus covered with fresh flowers. The patriarch read the last chapter of Matthew's gospel over the shroud, which was then reverently picked up and brought down to the stone of unction, where, after being processed around the stone three times, it was placed full length and then anointed with oils and wrapped in linen. These devotions were accompanied by prayers, psalms, and a short sermon. The figurative body having thus been prepared, the shroud was again borne aloft, this time to the Sepulchre, where it was laid to rest after processing three time around the tomb. The 'body' was then visited and kissed by the dignitaries before being sealed into the tomb, and finally around

3.00am the lights were extinguished [Graham, p. 277-283]. Jesus was in His tomb but the church, filled with expectant pilgrims, was still vibrantly alive.

The Sacred Fire ceremony itself began the next afternoon at 2.00pm The long wait and the preparatory procession all worked together to create heightened expectations and excitement. Graham claims that the Russians did not find the Sacred Fire central to the Easter ceremony, and yet they gathered there in great numbers and even had specially constructed boxes with two chambers, each containing a wick, so that they could transport the light from the Holy Fire back home. As the patriarch and the Armenian *vartabed*, both stripped of any robes which could conceal a flame, broke the seal and entered the tomb, the church filled with a sudden and eerie silence. Would it happen? Would the Fire appear? Was Christ really risen? These interrelated questions seemed to hang in the air. Finally out of the tomb came the lighted taper. All was well – the Easter celebrations could begin. At this point 'hundreds of pilgrims produced their black death-caps filled with sweet scented cotton-wool, and they extinguished the candles in them. These death-caps embroidered with bright silver crosses they proposed to keep to their death day and wear in the grave' [Graham, p. 290].

Following the Sacred Fire came the vigil, which ended with the Easter service at midnight in the Sepulchre; then finally the Russians would return for a service at the cathedral in the compound at 1.00am. Once this service was over the pilgrims went back to the hostel, where a real breaking of the fast was waiting for them and the lenten discipline gave way to feasting, dancing, and the return of alcohol, which most had given up for the duration [Graham, p. 296-297].

When the celebrating subsided, the pilgrims began to plan for the journey home. Last minute purchases were made and if possible shipped. Graham recounts one women who wanted a nearly life-sized madonna for her village. She convinced the shopkeeper to give it to her on deposit and then sat with the 'doll' on a busy street and begged for the money to make the purchase. In a few days she paid off her debt. Others picked up the olivewood crosses and similar souvenirs or 'blessings' and packed them in sacks to carry on the long trip home. But the heart if not the luggage seemed light because they had been to Jerusalem over Easter and they were the inheritors of a great promise that out of death would come life. Many brought a mark of their new found heavenly status home with them in the form of a tattoo on the arm to demonstrate to all that they were pilgrims – *hajjis*. (This Islamic term was picked up and used by the Christians.) The true rewards might be heavenly, but the status of a returned pilgrim in earthly Russia was not to be dismissed lightly. The most important treasures of the returning pilgrims, however, were the shroud and death-cap which would follow them into the grave. These would announce, at the very gates of heaven, that here was a person who was no stranger, but someone who by visiting the earthly Jerusalem was a citizen of the heavenly one.

What were the Russians' expectations, how were these realized or disappointed and what was the theological significance of Jerusalem?

The Russian pilgrims expected the Holy Land to be like the Jerusalem pictured in the divine liturgy and in their icons. And to the extent that Orthodox spirituality had been shaping the Holy Sites for centuries and turning them into icons of the spiritual mysteries they represented, these expectations were largely met. That which most alienated the Protestants is what the Russian Orthodox both demanded and got. The Russians wanted the Holy Places to be encrusted with the rites and iconography of their faith. They did not want only the human Palestine nor only the human Jesus; for them, it was the Nestorian heresy to see the human Jesus separated or separable from the divine. The Russian peasants, of course, did not express their views in these theological terms, but the same instincts were operative.

The Palestine these Russian pilgrims sought, just as the Jesus they sought, was a salvific combination of divine and human. It was this mystery which they came to contemplate, and the sites were expected to reflect and proclaim that mystery. After all the cave within which God became man is not a cave like any other, and in order to proclaim the 'reality' of that holy spot, the cave needed to be marked out and its inherent glory symbolized. It is extraordinary and needed to radiate that status to the blinded eyes of the world. Similarly the Life-Giving Tomb of Jesus is not a mere geographical spot but a place of cosmic significance. The world of divine reality broke in at this spot and the structure of reality – its ontological nature – was altered forever. Such a reality would not be adequately represented by a tomb which looks like a tomb because then the reality of this Life Giving-Tomb would be obscured rather than revealed. So the Tomb of Christ, like the manger, needed to be made into an icon which does not physically describe but rather uncovers the spiritual truth and in doing so puts the worshipper in contact with the divine energy that lies within and behind the object.

Speaking of Byzantine pilgrims, Gary Vikan describes the experience of being in the Holy Sepulchre:

> The Sepulchre itself converged for a moment to form a 'living icon' of the Resurrection. For like an icon, they [the worshippers], by virtue of the iconographic verisimilitude, collectively joined that chain of imparted sanctity leading back to their archetype, to the biblical event itself. And in doing so they accomplished what Theodore the Studite said all artificial images achieved: 'Every artificial image . . . exhibits in itself, by way of imitation, the form of its model . . . the model [is] in the image the one in the other.' Thus these pilgrims did not merely touch the locus sanctus, they became, at least briefly, iconically one and the same with it, and with that sacred event which had made it holy. [Gary Vikan, 'Pilgrims in Magi's Clothing: The Impact of Mimesis on Early Byzantine Pilgrimage Art', *The Blessings of Pilgrimage*, ed. Robert Ousterhout].

This Byzantine experience was appropriated by the Russian Church as well.

The Protestants saw the Holy Places and were distraught at how they had been altered from the simplicity of the biblical picture, whereas the Orthodox were uninterested in keeping the *loca sancta* historically pure. It is not the locus itself that is holy, but what had happened there that made it holy, so it is the significance of the locus that is represented. One example of this interconnection between the icons, the Holy Places, and the theological truths represented can be seen in the crucifixion icon of *ca.*1600 by the Russian School.

In this icon Christ crucified stands in the centre of the composition with the traditional disposition of the two Marys and John and a soldier at either side. At the base of the hill of calvary is a fissure, below which opens up a gap containing the skull of Adam and then widening into a deep black pit. Behind Jesus is a crenellated building or wall. The informed reader of this icon immediately understands the symbolism of Jesus being crucified over the skull of Adam because it is as the New Adam that He will re-create the world. And the black pit of hell is where the power of the cross will reach when the resurrected Christ visits that spot to bring life out of death. The walled Jerusalem which is both the city of sorrow and the city of joy represents the transformation of the human community into the divine community.

When observers of this or any one of thousands of icons like it visited Jerusalem, what did they find? They discovered Calvary to be a small hill supplanted with an icon of the crucifixion; below it they saw a fissure, and they would have the place of Adam's skull pointed out to them. They also saw the edicule of the Holy Sepulchre, shaped much like the backdrop of this icon, standing in the background. The story told in the icon and the story told at the Holy Site would connect because they both drew upon a common iconographic vocabulary and because behind both of them was the theological truth that Jesus' crucifixion had redeemed the sons of Adam from death. The icons, the divine liturgy, and the Holy Sites all were proclaiming one essentially interconnected gospel for those with eyes to see, for those with ears to hear, and for those with faith to understand.

Similarly, the Protestant quest for the historical Jesus or at least the human Jesus, which motivated so many of the English pilgrims, was considered by the Orthodox as a misconceived project. In his *The Mystical Theology of the Eastern Church*, Lossky says of the Western interest in the historical Jesus:

> The 'historical Jesus Christ', 'Jesus of Nazareth', as He appears to the eyes of alien witnesses; this image of Christ, external to the Church, is always surpassed in the fullness of the revelation given to the true witnesses, to the sons of the Church, enlightened by the Holy Spirit. The cult of the humanity of Christ is foreign to Eastern tradition; or rather this deified humanity always assumes for the Orthodox Christian that same glorious form under which it appeared to the disciples on Mt Tabor [Lossky, p. 243].

Whereas many Protestants, especially in the latter half of the nineteenth century, were searching for the human Jesus, the Orthodox were in quest of an equally biblical Jesus – the one of the Transfiguration and St John's Gospel – the Jesus whose divinity shone brightly through the flesh for those with the eyes of faith.

The Protestants were also acutely sensitive to the problems presented to the faith by an awareness of human historicity. David Hume's *Dialogues Concerning Natural Religion* (1779) had questioned whether any historical testimony could be an adequate reason for believing miracles, and historical studies were beginning to alert people to the historical nature of Christian doctrine and of the Bible itself. The corrosive effects of this developing historical consciousness on confidence in the truth of the Bible were, for many, of crisis proportions. These Protestants realized that their connection as residents of nineteenth-century Britain to the Jesus of first-century Palestine was problematic. The traditional route to Jesus was through the sacred text – the Bible – but that was becoming increasingly difficult as confidence in the historical accuracy of the text was questioned. The other route was that of religious experience, wherein the Jesus who transcends time is available through faith. But this Jesus, disconnected from history, became a mythic Jesus who seemed to lack reality. So for these

Protestants the Holy Land was a place to try to recapture the historical Jesus, or at least the biblical Jesus, and then like the disciples confront Him and hopefully, like them, find faith.

For the Orthodox, however, there are places where the eternal and the temporal intersect and where in a partial way the human, with all his faults, sins, and limitations, can partake in the heavenly realm. Most specifically this takes place in the Church during the divine liturgy. But if the divine liturgy is in its way the manifestation of the New Jerusalem, it is also true that at Easter in the Holy Sepulchre the Old Jerusalem and the New Jerusalem are united in an exceptional way. What happens is not just the representation of the first Easter, although this exists and is important; nor is it only that the eschatological community is gathered around the heavenly throne in an ecstasy of praise, although that is also present; and it is not merely the experiencing of the presence of Christ in the Eucharist, with the effects on body and soul that experience produces. In fact, all of these elements are combined – past, present, and future; man and God; history and eternity – in one glorious place and time. The Russian Orthodox pilgrim did not worry about problems of historicity because God had broken through time and finitude so that we could do the same.

One way of seeing this Orthodox transcendence of time into an eternity where everything is simultaneously present is to look at the liturgical texts for the various feast days. For example the text for Good Friday is:

> Today He who is by nature unapproachable, becomes approachable for me, and suffers His Passion, thus setting me free from passion.

And the Annunciation text reads:

> Today is revealed the mystery that is from all eternity. The Son of God becomes the Son of man, that, sharing what is worse, He makes me share what is better. In times of old Adam was once deceived; he sought to become God, but received not his desire. Now God

becomes man, that He might make Adam God . . . O
Marvel! God is come among men, who cannot be
contained is contained in a womb, the timeless enters
time . . .

Each of these texts is in the present tense, expressing the
conviction that these are not events relegated to the past,
inaccessible except through memory. These mysterious acts of God
are in fact eternally present and available to be entered into through
the Church.

So the liturgy, the icons, and the Holy Places are not only
windows into eternity, but doors as well because one can pass over
the threshold, and what one sees can also be participated in. So that
which is represented and symbolized is also, to the faithful, available
because it is re-presented, made present once again.

It is this effectual nature of the Holy Places as channels of grace
which distinguishes the Orthodox view of the Holy Land from that
of the English Protestants and explains why the Russians were so
determined to go there. In his article on Byzantium, Henri
Gregorie sums up the spirit which motivated the Russian pilgrims:

> Christians were Christians only because Christianity
> brought them liberation from death. If one would
> penetrate to the heart of Eastern Christianity one must
> be present on the night when the Easter liturgy is
> celebrated; of this liturgy all other rites are but reflections
> or figures. The three words of the Easter troparion – the
> Easter hymn – repeated a thousand times in tones ever
> more and more triumphant, repeated to the point of
> ecstasy and of an overflowing mystical joy – 'By His
> death He has trodden death beneath His feet' – here is
> the great message of the Byzantine Church [quoted in
> Meyendorff, p. 212].

And to be able to participate in the celebration and re-
presentation of that victory over death on the very site where it
happened, so that the victory would be theirs as well – this was what

the Russian pilgrims sought in Jerusalem. In the words of the hymn quoted partially above, 'Christ is risen from the dead having trodden death by his death and having granted life to those in the tombs.' This new life is what they wanted to celebrate and what they wanted to appropriate. The importance of Jerusalem, therefore, was as a source of salvific grace and as a journey to the earthly Jerusalem in preparation for the journey to the heavenly one.

The Russian Political Agenda

It may seem crass and anti-climatic to descend from the spiritual heights of the previous section to consider the political motives and implications of the Russian pilgrimage. But such is the nature of religion in the Holy Land that the sublime coexists with and in fact is inseparable from the material, commercial, and political machinations of human beings. The vast majority of Russian pilgrims, of course, went through their experience without an overtly political programme. They were, after all, in search of the heavenly Jerusalem, not the earthly one. But equally 'the Holy Land was as dear to the Slav soul as to the people who lived in Palestine' [Stavrou, p. 100]. And even the most politically naive pilgrim could not avoid noticing that the Holy Land was under Turkish and therefore infidel administration. They saw that Christians, both pilgrims and the native congregations (predominantly Orthodox), were under strict regulations and occasional persecutions. They brought back with them this scandal of the Holy Places being under Islamic political control, as well as the lesser though no less galling impudence of the Latin, Protestant, and heretical Eastern Churches having a visible presence in Jerusalem.

There was little doubt in the mind of the Russian peasant that the sites of the holy mysteries of the Church should be under the control of Mother Russia, the protector of the Orthodox faith. That this natural order did not apply in the very land of Christ was a source of sorrow and comment, although usually not of political intrigue. Disquiet with the situation, however, did provide a considerable body of public opinion which could be mobilized and exploited by leaders of Church and state in order to further a political goal when it was deemed desirable. The real political agenda of the Russian Church, therefore, tended to be found not among the illiterate peasants but among the policy-makers at the foreign ministry or Holy Synod in St Petersburg.

As we have already seen, when discussing why the pilgrims went to the Holy Land, there was a general agreement that sending a large contingent of Russian pilgrims to Palestine was in the political interests of both the Russian state and the Church. There was less agreement and, therefore, less consistency on other aspects of Russian presence in the Holy Land. The source of these differences seems to lie in the various fundamental concerns which motivated policy-makers. Some were primarily interested in geopolitical issues and therefore tended to vacillate between working to prop up the Ottoman empire and trying to tear it apart, depending upon which was seen as best promoting Russian territorial and commercial interests at the time. Others were motivated by a desire to free fellow Slavs from the yoke of Islamic Ottoman rule and calculated accordingly; these were the Pan-Slavs. Still others were interested in promoting Russia as the leader and liberator of the Orthodox Christian, especially those under Ottoman rule; these were the Pan-Orthodox. This last group differed from the Pan-Slavs by having a more consciously religious rather than ethnic based perspective and including the Orthodox Arabs in Palestine among those whose interests and liberation were paramount. Government and sometimes Church policy would depend upon which of these groups was predominate at the time.

Occasionally the interests of two or even of all three of these groups would coincide for a short time. So, for example, when confronting the Sublime Porte was part of the strategies of the geopolitical, the Pan-Slavic, and the Pan-Orthodox parties, they could agree on a policy such as sending an ecclesiastical mission to Jerusalem which would speak up for Russian interests. But that unanimity would soon break down over disagreements on how confrontational the representative should be and whether he should work with, against, or around the Greek Orthodox Patriarch of Jerusalem. The patriarch was, after all, ultimately accountable to both the sultan in Istanbul and his own Greek brotherhood in Jerusalem and was not eager for another constituency to please. Because the different parties disagreed on these strategic questions, chaos was created in the Russian institutions meant to implement policy in Palestine.

There was also confusion about the goals even at the very heart of the government. While the Russian foreign minister, Count Nesselrode, was developing a policy of supporting the tottering Ottoman empire after the death of Alexander I (1825), the Tsar, Nicholas I, wrote about his desire to conquer the Holy Land. This vacillation of policy between and within parties and even individuals all helped to spread confusion among the Russian community as well as foreign observers in Jerusalem, ultimately weakening Russian political influence in the region [Hopwood, p. 6-7].

Despite this nearly fatal weakness, the Russians were perceived as advancing in Palestine to the extent that many observers among the English Protestants, for example Tweedie, felt they might soon control the land itself as well as the sites. The pilgrims, with their vast numerical presence and the huge complex around the Russian cathedral to cater to their needs, helped foster this view. The other major factor was the establishment of schools, hospitals, and other charitable institutions among the native Arab Orthodox population. Created initially to parry the Protestant as well as French Catholic expansion in these areas and as a challenge to the authority of the Greek patriarch, these Russian institutions planted an abiding respect for and acquaintance with Russian language and culture among those who benefited. One can still meet in Jerusalem those who are thankful that their families were touched by these Russian charities.

The political and military power, geographic proximity, and religious concern of Russia, as well as the weakness of the Ottoman empire, all pointed towards the logic of Russian expansion into the Holy Land. The desire of the Western powers, especially Britain, to see her excluded, the vacillation and confusion of her policies and policy-makers, and the collapse of the Russian empire to Communism before the demise of the Ottomans dashed Russian political hopes and dreams. This Russian vacuum created after

World War I left the field open for the British and French mandates. The success of the Communists also put an end to the ubiquitous Russian pilgrims. Only now, with the collapse of Communism at the end of the 1980s, is there talk of the return of the Russians as pilgrims not ideologues or Jewish emigrés. If they do return, it will most likely be, as in the 19th century, primarily to partake in that spiritual grace which prayerful attendance at the Holy Sites bestows. And it will also probably be the case that someone will try to exploit the political potential of pilgrimage.

Conclusion

One facet of the Protestant/Orthodox conflict over the nature and efficacy of the Holy Places can be traced back to the Christian community's earliest struggle with the importance of the Holy Land. In his book *The Land Called Holy*, Robert Wilken initially focuses on Justin and Irenaeus, who view the physical land as having an eschatological role, a place where God's new kingdom will be inaugurated. The interpretation of these two Church Fathers is in contrast to Origen's view that the physical land serves primarily as a commentary on the scriptures. For Origen the eschatological land is to be understood allegorically to mean the kingdom of God. This Origenian use of the Holy Land as a place which could provide an historical and geographical context for explicating Scriptures was also the primary understanding of Jerome and Eusebius of Caesarea. Egeria's pilgrimage in the late fourth century shares this particular patristic outlook, exemplified by her habit of reading the appropriate scriptural texts at the numerous Old and New Testament sites she visits. But, Wilken notes, when she arrives in Jerusalem she is less interested in the sites as a backdrop for a scriptural text; instead she enters into the rituals of the place. There was arising, he contends, a 'tactile piety . . . holiness was being transferred through touching' [Wilken, p. 116].

Sabine MacCormack, in her article 'Loca Sancta', argues that the early Christian view of the Holy Land as providing an enhancement for biblical texts and evidence for their truth (empty tomb) became in time connected with allegorical and spiritualizing trends, which then reinforced each other so that the Tomb of Christ, which marked the central and definitive event of world history, came to be perceived as the geographical centre of the world. In the same way the death of Christ on Calvary, which reverses the sin of Adam, was understood as taking place over Adam's skull. Following from this intertwined historical and allegorical interpretation of the Holy Sites, they also accrued (around the sixth century) miraculous powers.

> The holy places in turn no longer acted merely as mementos for and monuments of the events told in Scripture. Rather the holy places sent forth a beneficent shower of miracles – that is, the holiness or sacred energy that was inherent in the place . . . [MacCormack, p. 26].

The tension of the land as historical and allegorical, as memorial and as miracle, was recognized by Gregory of Nyssa, who on the one hand critiqued those pilgrims who thought God was in one place more than another, and yet recognized that:

> if God had once been present on earth in Jesus of Nazareth, the soil on which he walked, the cave in which he was born, the stones of the tomb in which he was buried bear the imprint of God's presence and are, in the words of John of Damascus, 'receptacles of divine energy' [Wilken, p. 117-119].

So the Orthodox theology of the Holy Land, like its theology of the icon, was ultimately based upon the mystery of the Incarnation. If God became man, then the transcendent is not equally present, everywhere because in one person God was uniquely present and at certain places that unique incarnate God dwelt while living among humankind.

The collapse of the intertwined historical, allegorical, memorial and miraculous aspects of the Holy Land began in the West with the separation of the historical and the allegorical during the Renaissance and the Age of Exploration. With the development of world trade and the concomitant need for more accurate maps, it became increasingly difficult to maintain, for example, that Jerusalem was the geographical centre of earth. The historical centrality of Jerusalem was separated from its geographical position. The separation of the memorial from the miraculous was also an important component of Reformation theology, especially that of Zwingli and Calvin. Those reformers who understood the Eucharist as a memorial and not a miracle would not condone the connection between memorial and miracle in Holy Places, either local saints' shrines or those sites in far away Jerusalem. But the most devastating critique of this interconnection came from Hume and the Enlightenment. Miracles were henceforth exiled from the developing scientific worldview.

But despite the Westernization of Peter the Great, neither the Renaissance, Reformation, nor the Enlightenment were an integral part of the Russian intellectual heritage. Therefore, the interconnected nature of history and allegory and of memorial and miracle continued to inform how the Russians understood the Holy Land. In the nineteenth century this difference was understood by the West as a result of the failure of the Eastern Christians to have advanced or evolved through the inevitable steps that led to modern thought; eventually they too would follow the Western path into purer, more objective, more spiritualized truth. The Protestant missionaries especially evidenced this perspective.

When, therefore, the English Protestants encountered Orthodox Jerusalem, they saw it as an opportunity for bringing their deluded brothers into the modern world with modern technology, modern education, and a modern interpretation of Christianity. This modern Christianity, they confidently believed, more accurately captured the primitive faith of the Apostles. They believed that if they could return to the simple Jesus of the Holy Land, then the Holy Land would be returned to Jesus – and Jews, Muslims and Orthodox would see the light. The Orthodox, seeing the Protestant dismissal of ancient tradition, feared that the Incarnate Jesus Christ,

God made man, was being replaced by the man Jesus whose divine characteristics were rejected as pious legend and impossible miracles. They feared that the Orthodox Jesus was being replaced, in fact, by a Nestorian one. Neither understood the piety, the iconography, the sacramentality, the theological fears or the theological paradigms of the other.

But to say that the English Protestants and the Russian Orthodox were two communities speaking different theological and iconographic languages is only part of the story. As we have seen, these different approaches to the Holy Land harkened back to the very origins of Christianity. Although one group or another might put the emphasis upon the land as either scriptural exegete or conduit of holy power, the two aspects seem to be linked. The Russian Orthodox might emphasize the sacred power, the iconic identification of the place with the event, the symbol with the archetype, but it is the biblical story – the narrative – which makes sense of it all. And it is the biblical story which is read or liturgically represented at the sites. Similarly, as much as the Protestants attempt to trivialize the significance of the place, they are nonetheless enthralled by the power of the land to vivify the story. They assert that every place has equal access to the divine grace, but they endure hardship to travel to the Holy Land, they recommend it as part of a theological education, they make the experience available to those at home through books and pictures, they call it the 'fifth gospel' or other Bible. The power of the place seizes them, and they search for a suitable language to express that experience adequately.

This is not to ignore or devalue the wide gulf that separates the two experiences, but it is to claim that they are not, in the terminology of Thomas Kuhn, operating from two incommensurate paradigms. Although they may rarely have understood each other, the English Protestants and the Russian Orthodox pilgrims of the nineteenth century are not in fact speaking two foreign and incomprehensible languages. They are communicating in two dialects of the same language, sharing the one underlying faith in the person whose earthly home they find so enchanting.

Bibliography

Baggley, John. *Doors of Perception: Icons and Their Spiritual Significance*, London: 1987.

Bartlett, W H. *Walks About The City and Environs of Jerusalem*, London: 1844.

Bell, Revd Charles D. *Gleanings From a Tour in Palestine and The East*, London: 1883.

Brendon, Piers. *Thomas Cook: 150 Years of Popular Tourism*, London: 1991.

Brinton, John. *Tour in Palestine and Syria*, London: 1893.

Carradine, Revd Beverly. *A Journey to Palestine*, St.Louis: 1891.

Charley, Sir Charles. *The Holy City*, London: 1902.

Clark, Francis and Harriet. *Our Journey Around The World*, Hartford: 1895.

Condor, *Tent Works*, London: 1878.

Cunningham, James. *Pilgrims in Palestine*, Edinburgh: 1905.

Cuthbertson, James. *Sacred and Historic Lands*, London: 1855.

Dmitrievskii, D S. *O Russkom Palomnichestve i Imperatorskom Pravoslavno m Palestinskom Obshchestve*, St. Petersburg: 1899.

Davies, J G. *Pilgrimage Yesterday and Today. Why? Where? How?* London: 1988.

Durbin, John. *Observations in The East*, New York: 1845.

Gadsby, John. *My Wanderings: Being Travels in The East in 1846-47, 1850-51, 1852-53*, London: 1881.

Graham, Stephen. *With the Russian Pilgrims to Jerusalem*, London: 1913.

Gray, Andrew. *A Pilgrimage to Bible Lands*, London: 1903.

Hannington, James. *The Last Journals of Bishop James Hannington*, edited by E.C. Dawson, London: 1888.

Hertslet, Reginald. *Jerusalem and the Holy Land in 1882*, London: 1883.

Hopwood, Derick. *Russian Presence in Syria and Palestine: 1843-1914*, Oxford: 1969.

Jowett, William. *Christian Researches in Syria and the Holy Land*, London: 1825.

Kabbani, Rana. *Europe's Myths of Orient*, London: 1986.

Keith, Alexander. *Evidence of The Truth of The Christian Religion, Derived From the Literal Fulfilment of Prophecy; Particularly as Illustrated By the History of the Jews, and By The Discoveries of Recent Travellers*, Edinburgh: 1832.

Kelman, John. *The Holy Land*, London: 1904.

Khitrovo, V N. *Russkie Palomniki Sviatoi Zemli*, St. Petersburg: 1896.

King, Mrs. *Dr. Liddon's Tour in Egypt and Palestine in 1886*, London: 1891.

Leach, Charles, MP. *The Romance of the Holy Land*, London: 1911.

Leighton, William H. *A Cook's Tour to the Holy Land in 1874*, London: 1947.

Lent, William. *Holy Land From Landau, Saddle and Palanquin*, New York: 1899.

Lossky, Vladimir. *The Mystical Theology of the Eastern Church*, Cambridge: 1991.

Luke, Henry Charles. *Ceremonies at the Holy Places*, London: 1932.

Martin, Eustace M. *A Visit to the Holy Land, Syria and Constantinople*, London: 1883.

Meen, Joseph. *Geography of Palestine*, London: 1860.

Mikhailovskii, V I. *Sputnik Provoslavnago Poklonnika v Sviatuiu Zemliu*, St. Petersburg: 1886-87.

Miller, William. *The Least of All Lands*, London: 1888.

Meyendorff, John. *Byzantine Theology: Historical Trends and Doctrinal Themes*, London: 1974.

Neil, C Lang. *Rambles in Bible Lands*, London: 1905.

Neil, Henry. *Neil's Photographs of the Holy Land*, Philadelphia: 1893.

Neil, Revd James. *Palestine Explored*, London: 1882.

Olin, Revd Stephen. *Travels in Egypt, Arabia, Petra, and the Holy Land*, New York: 1843.

Osborn, Revd Henry. *The Pilgrim in the Holy Land*, London: 1860.

Otts, J M P. *The Fifth Gospel: The Land Where Jesus Lived*, London: 1893.

Ousterhout, Robert, ed. *The Blessings of Pilgrimage*, Urbana: 1990.

Paxton, Revd J D. *Letters from Palestine*, London: 1839.

Pelikan, Jaroslav. *The Spirit of Eastern Christendom (600-1700)*, Vol. 2 of *The Christian Tradition*, Chicago: 1977.

Ridgway, Revd James. *Sketches From the East: Illustrating Church Doctrine and Practice*, Oxford: 1893.

Schaff, Philip. *Through Bible Lands*, London: 1889.

Shaffer, E S. *'Kubla Khan' and the Fall of Jerusalem: The Mythological School in Biblical Criticism and Secular Literature 1770-1880*, Cambridge: 1975.

Shepherd, Naomi. *The Zealous Intruders: The Western Rediscovery of Palestine*, London: 1987.

Stanley, A P. *Sinai and Palestine*, London: 1910.

Stavrou, Theofanis George. *Russian Interests in Palestine: 1882-1914*, Institute for Balkan Studies: 1963.

Taylor, Bayard. *The Land of the Saracen*, New York: 1857.

Thomas, Revd Joseph. *Oxford to Palestine*, London: 1890.

Thomson, W M. *The Land and the Book*, London: 1870.

Tibawi, A L. *British Interests in Palestine: 1800-1901*, Oxford: 1961.

Treves, Sir Frederick. *The Land That is Desolate: An Account of a Tour in Palestine*, London: 1913.

Turner, Victor and Edith. *Image and Pilgrimage in Christian Culture*, Oxford: 1978.

Tweedie, Revd W K. *Jerusalem and Its Environs*, London: 1873.

Warburton, Eliot. *The Crescent and the Cross*, London: 1845.

Ware, Timothy. *The Orthodox Church*, London: 1964.

Warner, Charles Dudley. *In the Levant*, Boston: 1877.

Wilken, Robert L. *The Land Called Holy*, New Haven: 1992.

Wybrew, Hugh. *The Orthodox Liturgy*, London: 1990.

Yannaras, Christos. *Elements of Faith: An Introduction to Orthodox Theology*, Edinburgh: 1991.

Chronology

1799   Napoleon's expedition to Egypt and Palestine

1808   London Society for Promoting Christianity among the Jews

1829   Treaty of Adrianople recognizes Russia as guardian of Orthodox Christian population of the Ottoman Empire

1831   Mohammed Ali and Ibrahim Pasha of Egypt rule Jerusalem until 1839

1838   British Consulate established

1839   First daguerreotypes produced outside of Europe taken in Middle East; Tanzimat reforms in the Ottoman Empire

1841   Creation of the joint Anglican-Prussian Bishopric in Jerusalem

1844   American Consulate established

1848   Russian Ecclesiastical Mission established (disbanded in 1854 during the Crimean War)

1853-56   Crimean War

1858   Russian Consulate established

1857   Land outside of the city wall purchased for building the Russian Compound; Second Russian Ecclesiastical Mission

1864   Russian Compound at this point consists of three hospices, a hospital, the Cathedral and the consulate building

1869   Suez Canal opened; first paved road between Jaffa and Jerusalem; first Cook's Tour to the Holy Land; Palestine Exploration Fund established in London

1882   Russian Orthodox Palestine Society replaces Palestine Committee

1892   Jaffa to Jerusalem railroad inaugurated

1914   World War I and the end of Russian pilgrimage

1917   Britain occupies Jerusalem, 400 years of Ottoman control ended

Index